KENNET AND AVON CANAL

THE FULL CANAL WALK
AND 20 DAY WALKS

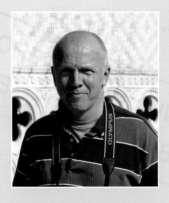

About the Author

Steve Davison is a writer and photographer who has lived in Berkshire for over 25 years. He has written a number of books, as well as articles for outdoor magazines and other publications, including local and national newspapers. He specialises in hillwalking and European travel, with interests in nature, geology and the countryside. A keen hillwalker for many years and a Mountain Leader, Steve has also worked as a part-time outdoor education instructor. He is a member of the Outdoor Writers and Photographers Guild. Find out more about him at www.steve-davison.co.uk.

Other Cicerone guides by the author

Walking in the North Wessex Downs
The Great Stones Way
Walking in the Chilterns
The Ridgeway National Trail
Walking in the New Forest
Walking in the Thames Valley

THE KENNET AND AVON CANAL

THE FULL CANAL WALK
AND 20 DAY WALKS

by Steve Davison

2 POLICE SQUARE, MILNTHORPE, CUMBRIA LA7 7PY
www.cicerone.co.uk

© Steve Davison 2016
First edition 2016
ISBN: 978 1 85284 786 9

Printed by KHL Printing, Singapore
A catalogue record for this book is available from the British Library.

© Crown copyright 2016
OS PU100012932

All photographs are by the author unless otherwise stated.

Front cover: A narrowboat negotiates Wire Lock (76), between Kintbury and Hungerford (Stage 2, Walk 6)

CONTENTS

Route symbols on OS map extracts
(for OS legend see printed OS maps)

〰	main route
〰	alternative route/detour
🚶	start/finish point
🚶	start point
🚶	finish point
🚶	alternative start/finish point
🚶	alternative start
◀	route direction
🚴 4	on-road cycle route
4	off-road (traffic-free) cycle route

Features on the overview map

———	County/Unitary boundary
	Urban area

800m
600m
400m
200m
75m
0m

Heading through fields following the River Avon towards Keynsham (Stage 7)

7

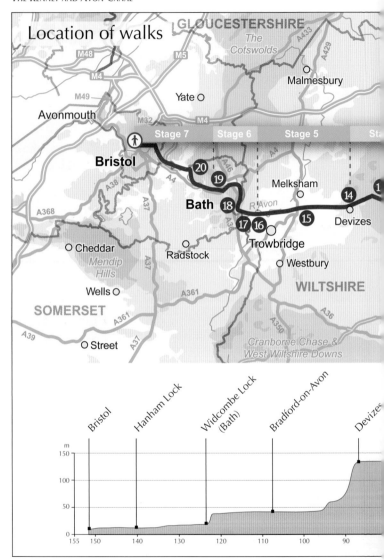

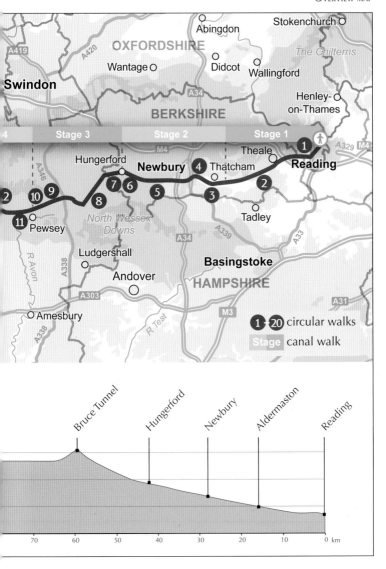

Caen Hill flight of locks ((Stage 5, Walk 14)

INTRODUCTION

The thatched Royal Oak pub at Wootton Rivers (Stage 3, Walk 9)

At the height of 'canal mania' in the early 1800s, the Kennet and Avon Canal, which stretches across southern England from Reading to Bristol, formed a super-highway for the transportation of goods ranging from coal and timber to grain and stone, contributing to the late Georgian and early Victorian growth of the south. However, the widespread use of the canal lasted only a few decades before the arrival of Isambard Kingdom Brunel's much faster Great Western Railway.

The loss of business caused by the railways brought about a gradual decline of the canal system and by the 1950s the Kennet and Avon was in a very poor state. However, plans to abandon the canal were brushed aside by public support and an army of volunteers set about the gradual restoration of the canal, culminating in its reopening by Queen Elizabeth II in 1990.

Now this wonderful canal, which celebrated its bicentenary in 2010, forms a multi-faceted jewel for boaters, walkers and wildlife, as it weaves its way through a patchwork of countryside from the rolling chalk contours of the North Wessex Downs to the southern edge of the Cotswolds, passing vibrant towns and cities as well as picture-postcard villages with thatched cottages, ancient churches and cosy pubs.

Walking along the canal also takes you on a journey of discovery past impressive historical features including the world-famous Crofton Pumping Station and Beam Engines, the stunning Caen Hill flight of locks at Devizes, the ornate aqueducts at Avoncliff and Dundas, and the Georgian splendour of Bath.

But, most importantly in today's busy world, the canal offers an abundance of peace and tranquillity, a slower pace of life, where you are surrounded by a wide range of wildlife. As you walk, you are accompanied by the sounds of birdsong, the wind rustling through the trees, or a narrowboat chugging by, gently rippling the tranquil waters.

Whether you opt for walking the full length of the canal from Reading to Bristol's vibrant Floating Harbour (152.1km/94½ miles in total) or go for the 20 circular walks that take in the best sections of the canal while visiting interesting places nearby, this guidebook takes you on a fascinating journey across southern England, following one of England's best-loved canals.

To learn more about the volunteers who helped save this magical canal, visit the website of the Kennet & Avon Canal Trust (www. katrust.org.uk); to learn more about the work of the Canal & River Trust, who look after the waterways of England and Wales, visit their website (www.canalrivertrust.org.uk).

The canal passes the former Simonds' Brewery site in Reading (Stage 1)

BRIEF HISTORY OF THE CANAL

The Kennet and Avon Canal, which celebrated its bicentenary in 2010, was formed in the 19th century when two waterways – the Kennet Navigation and the Avon Navigation – were joined by the construction of a 91.5km (57 mile) canal between Newbury and Bath.

The 31.3km (19½ mile) Kennet Navigation, which ran from the River Thames at Reading to Newbury, opened in 1723. Designed by the Newbury engineer John Hore (1690–1762), the Kennet Navigation comprised sections of natural river and 18.5km (11½ miles) of new cut canal with 20 turf-sided locks, two of which survive today: Garston Lock and Monkey Marsh Lock.

The Avon Navigation, between Bath and Bristol, was opened in 1727 and incorporated six locks along the 18km (11 mile) section from Bath to Hanham (Hanham Lock is lock 1 of the Kennet and Avon Canal); downstream of Hanham the River Avon is tidal. Ralph Allen, previously postmaster of Bath, was one of the men instrumental in the opening of the Avon Navigation – he had bought stone mines at Combe Down and Bathampton and it was much easier to transport stone by barge than packhorse. As with the Kennet Navigation, the chief engineer was John Hore.

By 1770, people were starting to put forward the idea of building a canal that would link the River Kennet and the River Avon. Originally a route from Hungerford via Ramsbury and Marlborough was proposed. However, because of growing fears about the availability of a good supply of water, a more southerly route was proposed in 1793, passing through Great Bedwyn and the Vale of Pewsey, with an extension canal to Marlborough. The drawback with this route was the need for a 4km (2½ mile) summit tunnel between Crofton and Burbage.

Plans for the extension to Marlborough were shelved and in 1794 the proposal received Royal Assent, with John Rennie being appointed chief engineer. A further survey recommended altering the route yet again, this time raising the summit by 12m in order to reduce the length of the tunnel – known as the Bruce Tunnel – to 459 metres. This would substantially decrease the cost and time required to construct the canal, even though more locks and a steam-driven pump would be required to raise water to the new canal summit.

Finally, in October 1794, work started on the canal. The section from Newbury to Kintbury opened in 1797, followed by Hungerford in 1798 and Great Bedwyn in 1799. The section west of Great Bedwyn, including the Caen Hill Locks, took a further 10 years to build. In 1810, the Kennet and Avon Canal was finally opened, giving a direct trade route between London and Bristol.

Widcombe Lock (7) at the former Thimble Mill, Bath (Stage 6, Walk 19)

For 40 years the canal prospered, transporting a range of goods to and from wharves built along the canal, but the passing of the Great Western Railway Act in 1835 led to the building of Isambard Kingdom Brunel's railway, which offered a faster and more efficient transport route between London and Bristol. In 1852, the Great Western Railway Company succeeded in buying the Kennet and Avon Canal, although on the proviso that it was kept open as a canal. However, they made little attempt to maintain the route over the next 100 years, leading to its gradual decline; they even offered traders preferential tolls to use the railway instead.

During World War II, with the threat of a German invasion, a series of General Headquarters Anti-Tank Lines (or GHQ Stop Lines) were devised. These utilised existing natural obstacles such as rivers and also man-made ones, including canals and railway embankments, supplemented by a vast number of pillboxes, anti-tank ditches and other obstacles. The primary purpose of these defences was to delay any invasion forces, although fortunately they were never used in combat. One of these lines, GHQ Stop Line Blue, utilised the near-derelict Kennet and Avon Canal and along the length of the canal there are many former pillboxes.

By 1955, the canal was in very poor condition, but plans to abandon it completely were thwarted by public opposition. The Kennet &

Avon Canal Trust purchased Crofton Pumping Station and Beam Engines from British Waterways in 1968, with the objective of restoring them to full working order, and two years later the steam engines were working again. Although electric pumps have been installed to pump water into the canal, these magnificent steam-driven beam engines are still used on several occasions throughout the year. The 1812 Boulton and Watt is the oldest working beam engine in the world.

The full length of the canal, restored and cared for by the Kennet & Avon Canal Trust, was formally reopened by Queen Elizabeth II in 1990. Nowadays the canal forms a popular heritage tourism destination for boating, walking and cycling as well as being an important feature for wildlife conservation. A selection of books that provide interesting further reading on the Kennet and Avon Canal are given in Appendix E.

GEOLOGY

The landscape through which the Kennet and Avon Canal travels tells the story of the seas that once covered southern England and the sediments that were laid down at that time. Due to movements within the earth's crust some 50 million years ago that gave rise to the Alps, these layers of sedimentary rocks, which lie with the older deposits at the bottom and the more recent ones at the top, now gently slope down to the south-east.

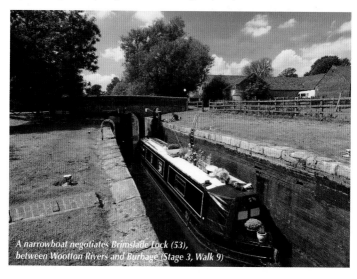

A narrowboat negotiates Brimslade Lock (53), between Wootton Rivers and Burbage (Stage 3, Walk 9)

This, combined with subsequent erosion, has allowed the older layers to be revealed in the west.

Throughout the eastern section of the canal, from Reading through the North Wessex Downs Area of Outstanding Natural Beauty (AONB) to Devizes, the predominant feature is a thick layer of Upper Cretaceous chalk (99–65 million years ago), composed of incredible numbers of tiny fossil skeletons of algae, called coccoliths. Associated with the upper (white) layer of chalk are horizontal bands of irregular silica concretions, known as flints; these also occur in profusion in the jumbled deposits of weathered chalk, known as 'clay-with-flints'. When struck, flint breaks with a shell-shaped fracture, leaving very sharp edges, and our Stone Age ancestors used flints to make arrowheads and hand axes. Being a very hard-wearing rock, flint has also been widely used as a building material.

Within the sandy beds that overlay the chalk, a natural process of patchy and irregular hardening produced blocks of tough sandstone, known as sarsens, that are more resistant to erosion. Sarsens can be seen on some of the walks to the west of Hungerford and above the Vale of Pewsey (especially Walk 12).

Underlying the porous chalk is a layer of greensand and impervious Gault clay, laid down during the latter part of the Lower Cretaceous period (140–99 million years ago). This layer of clay gives rise to a spring-line

Looking east, shortly after Crofton Pumping Station (Stage 3)

The River Kennet near Hamstead Lock (81) (Walk 5)

where water that has seeped through the chalk is forced to the surface to form springs, which become chalk rivers such as the River Kennet.

Further west in the southern reaches of the Cotswold Hills AONB, older layers of rock lie below the Gault clay. These layers include oolitic limestone (a buff-coloured rock that has been widely used as a building material throughout the Cotswolds), laid down during the Jurassic period (200–140 million years ago). Oolitic limestone is made up of ooids (small spherical grains composed of concentric layers) that form in shallow, warm sub-tropical seas where calcium carbonate is deposited from sea water due to evaporation. The tiny grains gradually grow in size as they are rolled around by wave action.

The area around Bath is home to a fine-grained oolitic limestone known locally as Bath stone. This was used extensively in the construction of many buildings in Bath as well as the Dundas and Avoncliff Aqueducts along the canal. Bath stone was first worked by the Romans and is still mined at Stoke Hill Mine, Limpley Stoke (Walk 17). Other areas where Bath stone was quarried include Monkton Farleigh and around Brown's Folly (itself made of Bath stone), where there are a number of interesting rock outcrops (Walk 18).

Looking west across the Avon Valley towards Monkton Combe (Stage 6, Walk 17)

Travelling further west to Bristol sees the appearance of the oldest rocks along the route, namely red sandstone from the Triassic period (250–200 million years ago). This fine-grained rock was mined in the Redcliffe area of Bristol between the 15th and 18th centuries for use in the glass industry. Pennant sandstone from the Upper Carboniferous (310–300 million years ago) has also been mined around Hanham and Troopers Hill.

Throughout the last 2.6 million years (the Quaternary period), Britain has been subject to periods of glaciation separated by warmer interglacial periods (the last glacial period ended about 12,000 years ago). There is no evidence to suggest that southern England was ever covered in ice, but the area did suffer periglacial conditions. In the chalk downs, this allowed the formation of dry valleys, which were eroded by water flowing over the surface during cold periods when the underlying ground was frozen, making the normally porous rock impermeable. During this geological period, rivers formed large gravel deposits, especially along the Kennet Valley, and these gave rise to the development of gravel extraction works. Many former gravel pits have been flooded to form wetland habitats and the canal passes a number of these between Reading and Newbury.

18

PLANTS AND WILDLIFE

Following the canal takes you on a journey through a patchwork landscape with areas of open grassland, broadleaved woodland and farmland.

Throughout the walks you should have plenty of opportunities for catching glimpses of local wildlife, from foxes to roe and fallow deer, or perhaps a badger as dusk approaches. Some of the walks cross areas of open chalk grasslands which support a wide range of butterflies, plants (including gentians and orchids) and birds such as the skylark and yellowhammer. You might see a buzzard or red kite soaring high above, silhouetted against the sky; the buzzard has a rounded tail whereas the red kite has a forked tail.

Alongside the canal and rivers, during the summer months, there

Clockwise from top left: damselfly; yellow flag iris; grey heron; common centaury; and mute swan (centre)

19

Bradford-on-Avon is one of the railway stations that can be used to access the canal (Stages 5 and 6, Walk 16)

are dragonflies, damselflies and butterflies as well as the ever-present ducks, coots, moorhens and mute swans. You may see great crested grebes, a grey heron patiently watching the water, waiting to catch a passing fish, or summer-visiting reed and sedge warblers, or spot the vivid turquoise-blue-and-orange flash of a kingfisher as it darts along the river. Maybe you will see the endangered water vole or, for the lucky few, an otter.

Waterside plants include the bright flowers of the yellow flag iris and stands of 1.5m-high common reed, which sometimes hide the canal from view. In the area around Bath, look out for the tall yellowish spikes of the nationally scarce Bath asparagus, also known as the spiked star of Bethlehem.

WHERE TO STAY

There is a wide range of accommodation, ranging from youth hostels and campsites to guesthouses, pubs with rooms, and hotels. The itinerary planner in Appendix B provides an overview of the different kinds of accommodation available at places near to the canal. Appendix C lists accommodation near to the route, including phone numbers and websites. To find out more about accommodation, visit the tourist information websites listed in Appendix D.

GETTING TO AND AROUND THE CANAL

A number of main roads cross the canal at various points, joining with either the A4 or the M4 (both of which take an east–west route between London, Reading and Bristol). If travelling by car to any of the walks or canal stages, always remember to park considerately and never block access routes.

Railway stations that can be used to give access to the canal include: Reading, Theale, Aldermaston Wharf (Aldermaston station), Woolhampton (Midgham station), Thatcham, Newbury, Kintbury, Hungerford, Great Bedwyn, Pewsey, Melksham (off route), Trowbridge (off route), Bradford-on-Avon, Avoncliff, Freshford (off route), Bath, Keynsham and Bristol (Temple Meads). Where a specific walk or stage may be accessed by train, the nearest railway stations are given in the corresponding information box. Some walks and stages may also be accessed using buses – brief details are provided in each information box. For the latest information relating to public transport, use the contact details in Appendix D.

FOOD AND DRINK

Some of the canal stages and walks start at places where food and drink may be bought, whether it's a shop, café or pub; some offer opportunities for stopping off en route at a pub or shop, although these are not always conveniently placed along the route. Brief details of refreshment opportunities are given in the information box at the start of each route, but bear in mind that there is no guarantee they'll be open when required. Therefore it's always a good idea to carry some food and drink with you, along with a small 'emergency ration' in case of an unexpected delay.

WALKING THE CANAL

This guide is in two parts: the first part covers the route along the entire length of the canal, while the second part describes 20 circular walks spaced along the length of the canal.

Walking the canal from Reading to Bristol

This section of the guide describes the route along the length of the canal. It has been split into seven stages ranging from 15.7 to 28.6km (9¾ to 17¾ miles), following the canal west from Reading to Bristol (see Appendix A for a stage summary table). Each stage may be further split into two convenient parts where there is parking and, in most cases, transport available. Suggestions for splitting the stages are given in the information box at the beginning of each stage.

For your own enjoyment and convenience, plan your walk carefully in advance. The stages are not intended to be individual day sections, but the start and end points coincide with places that offer parking and transport links locally and, within a reasonable distance, accommodation facilities (see Appendix B for an itinerary planner). The stages are provided to help walkers decide how far they would like to go each day, whether that means undertaking just part of a stage or combining multiple stages. It is entirely up to you how far you want to walk each day.

When following the stage descriptions, bear in mind that the locks decrease in number when travelling westwards from Blake's Lock (107) at Reading to Hanham Lock (1), whereas the bridges increase in number.

Circular walks

The 20 individual circular walks in this guide range from 6.8 to 15km (4¼ to 9¼ miles) and cover fairly low-level terrain (less than 286m above sea level). Although some walks have several climbs and descents, some of which are steep, they should be suitable for most walkers. The routes generally follow well-defined tracks and paths, although some paths may be narrow and at times indistinct. The walk summary table in Appendix A provides the key statistics for all 20 walks.

Planning for the weather

When planning your walk, bear in mind the weather. Summers tend to be fairly dry and mild. Spring and autumn offer some of the best walking conditions: spring and early summer herald new life along the canal, with colourful displays of flowers, abundant birdsong and many butterflies, while cool

The Cunning Man pub at Burghfield Bridge sits beside the canal (Stage 1)

autumn nights clothe the countryside in shades of russet, gold and brown. During the winter months, spells of rain can make some paths quite muddy and some routes may be impassable when rivers are flooded. However, walking on a clear, frosty winter's day can be a magical experience.

Always choose clothing suitable for the season, along with a waterproof jacket, comfortable and waterproof footwear and a comfortable rucksack. On wet days, gaiters or waterproof trousers can also be very useful. It's also worth carrying a basic first aid kit to deal with minor incidents.

Cycling along the canal between the aqueducts at Avoncliff and Dundas (Stage 6, Walk 17)

CYCLING THE CANAL

Large sections of the canal towpath between Reading and Bath form part of Route 4 of the National Cycle Network and have been improved accordingly. National Cycle Route 4 (NCR4) generally follows the River Kennet and canal from Reading (SU 730 738) to Thatcham railway station (SU 527 663). After 4.6km on urban roads through Thatcham, it rejoins the towpath at Ham Bridge (SU 490 671) and then continues mainly on the towpath to Marsh Benham (SU 423 670). The next section to Devizes (SU 018 623) mostly follows country lanes, before rejoining the canal towpath to Bath (ST 758 654). From Bath to Bristol, NCR4 follows the Bristol & Bath Railway Path. For a map of NCR4, visit the Sustrans website at www.sustrans.org.uk.

The map extracts in this guide show the National Cycle Route 4; this is denoted with a solid green circle for on-road and a green circle with white centre for off-road (traffic-free) parts of the route.

The latest advice from the Canal & River Trust is that considerate cycling is allowed alongside the canal from Reading to Bath (visit www.canalrivertrust.org.uk for more information). Between Bath and Bristol, cyclists should follow the Bristol & Bath Railway Path.

The whole length of the canal can be cycled over a two- or three-day period. A typical three-day itinerary might be:

- Day 1 – Reading to Hungerford: 45.6km (28¼ miles) via the towpath; add 3.1km (2 miles) via NCR4

23

- Day 2 – Hungerford to Bradford-on-Avon: 62.2km (38¾ miles) via the towpath; add 6.5km (4 miles) via NCR4
- Day 3 – Bradford-on-Avon to Bristol: 44.3km (27½ miles) via the towpath to Bath (which is also NCR4) and then following the Bristol & Bath Railway Path, which forms part of NCR4

When cycling along the towpath, please be courteous to walkers and other users, cycle more slowly, use a bell when approaching others and at bridges (proceed with caution) and dismount when passing through tunnels. Note that there is no towpath through the Bruce Tunnel, here the route diverts over the top of the tunnel.

MAPS

The Ordnance Survey (OS) offer two series of maps: the 1:50,000 (2cm to 1km) Landranger series and the more detailed 1:25,000 (4cm to 1km) Explorer series. The OS maps covering the canal and surrounding walks are:

- Landranger: 172, 173, 174 and 175
- Explorer: 155, 156, 157, 158 and 159

Other maps include Heron Maps: Kennet & Avon Canal and River Avon at 1:50,000 with detailed town plans at 1:12,500 (also shows National Cycle Route 4). This is only of use for walking the length of the canal, not for the 20 circular walks.

This guide features extracts from the OS 1:50,000 Landranger series of maps, with overlays showing the route along with any detours or shortcuts. It is advisable to always carry the relevant Explorer map with you when walking as these show much greater detail as to the routing of rights of way.

WAYMARKING, ACCESS AND RIGHTS OF WAY

The rights of way are typically well signposted using a mix of fingerposts, marker posts and waymarks on fences and gateposts; the towpath is very well signposted. The descriptions in this guide, in combination with the map extracts and the signage on the ground, should make route-finding straightforward; however, it is still advisable to carry a compass and the relevant OS Explorer map.

The routes in this guide follow official rights of way: footpaths, bridleways, restricted byways, and byways. Some routes also pass areas of open access land (marked on OS Explorer maps) where you can freely roam. Rights of way are marked as follows:

- **Footpaths** Yellow arrow – walkers only
- **Bridleways** Blue arrow – walkers, cyclists and horse riders
- **Restricted byways** Purple arrow – walkers, cyclists, horse riders and carriage drivers

Rights of way are usually well signposted

- **Byways** Red arrow – same as for a restricted byway plus motorcycles and motorised vehicles

Finally, always take extra care when either crossing or walking along roads, or when crossing railway lines.

PROTECTING THE COUNTRYSIDE

When out walking, please respect the countryside and follow the Countryside Code:

- Be safe – plan ahead and follow any signs.
- Leave gates and property as you find them.
- Protect plants and animals, and take your litter home.
- Keep dogs under close control.
- Consider other people.

Many of the walks pass through fields where cattle may be present. Follow the latest advice: do not walk between cows and young calves; if you feel threatened, move away calmly; do not panic or make sudden noises; and if possible find an alternative route.

USING THIS GUIDE

The descriptions in this guidebook all follow the same format. For the long route, an information box at the start of each stage description gives the start and finish locations accompanied by grid references; stage distance (km/miles) and cumulative distance; ascent in metres (m); minimum time required to complete the stage (hours); relevant maps; places that offer refreshments (pubs, cafés and shops) and accommodation; brief public transport information; and a suggestion of where the stage may be split. Some of the places suggested for refreshments, accommodation and public transport may be a short distance off the main route; for details, see the itinerary planner in Appendix B.

Following the canal back to Avoncliff (Stage 17)

The information boxes for the 20 short walks provide similar details to those of the stages, including brief details of where to park.

Each information box is followed by a short introduction to the stage or the walk, identifying any major points of interest, including villages. The route is then described in detail, with background information given for places of interest encountered along the way.

The map extracts are from the 1:50,000 OS Landranger series. Features shown on the map that are mentioned in the route are highlighted in bold text to help you follow the route.

The distances quoted for each walk (metric first, with approximate imperial conversions rounded to the nearest ¼, ½, ¾ or whole number) have been measured from OS Explorer maps: note that the heights quoted on the maps are in metres and the grid lines are spaced at intervals of 1 km. The walking time for each walk has been worked out using a walking speed of 4 km/hour (2½ miles/hour), plus 10 minutes for every 100 m of ascent. This should be treated as the absolute **minimum** amount of walking time required to undertake the walk and does not include any time for rests, photography, consulting the map or guidebook, or simply admiring the view – all of which can add substantially to the day's activity.

WALKING THE CANAL FROM READING TO BRISTOL

Dunmill Lock (75), just east of Hungerford (Stage 2)

STAGE 1
Reading to Woolhampton

Start	Kennet Mouth, Reading (SU 730 738)
Finish	Woolhampton Bridge (SU 572 665)
Distance	20.7km (12¾ miles); cumulative 20.7km (12¾ miles)
Total ascent	100m
Time	5½hr
Map	OS Explorer 159; Heron Maps: Kennet & Avon Canal
Refreshments	Reading, Burghfield Bridge, Theale, Tyle Mill, Aldermaston Wharf, Aldermaston, Woolhampton
Public transport	Railway stations at Reading, Theale, Aldermaston Wharf (Aldermaston station), Woolhampton (Midgham station); bus services at Reading, Burghfield Bridge, Theale, Tyle Mill, Ufton Bridge, Aldermaston Wharf, Woolhampton
Accommodation	Reading, Theale, Sulhamstead, Aldermaston Wharf, Aldermaston
Splitting the stage	The stage may be split after 11.2km (7 miles) at Theale (SU 647 704), where there is a railway station, parking and accommodation.

The first stage along the canal starts out from the River Thames and heads through the hustle and bustle of Reading town centre before passing into a more rural setting. After the M4 motorway, the route passes Garston Lock, one of only two turf-sided locks along the canal; along this part of the route there are several flooded gravel pits. After Theale, the route heads for Aldermaston Wharf, home to a small canal visitor centre and tea room, before continuing to the stage end at Woolhampton, beside the Rowbarge pub. For large parts of the stage, the canal and River Kennet flow as one.

From Reading railway station to the canal
Leave through the north (Caversham) exit, follow the signed walking/cycle route for Christchurch Meadows and Caversham past the bus stops, then across the A329 and along Norman Place to the River Thames. Turn right

along the Thames Path for 1.7km to the junction with the canal at Kennet Mouth. Follow the Thames Path over Horseshoe Bridge and turn sharp left, doubling back under the bridge to join the canal heading into Reading.

Reading was once home to a great abbey founded by Henry I in 1121 – now only sections of flint rubble walls remain. The playwright, poet and novelist Oscar Wilde was imprisoned at Reading Gaol in the late 1800s and following his release he wrote *The Ballad of Reading Gaol*. Reading Museum (0118 937 3400), housed in the Victorian Gothic Town Hall, charts the town's history and includes Roman artefacts from Calleva Atrebatum and a copy of the Bayeux Tapestry. (Walk 1 takes in the abbey ruins, the site of Reading Gaol, the Town Hall and Museum, and explores other locations in Reading.)

The town is often known for the 'Three Bs' of Beer, Bulbs and Biscuits, relating to three former industries that originated in the town: Simonds' Brewery, established by William Blackall Simonds in 1785; Suttons Seeds,

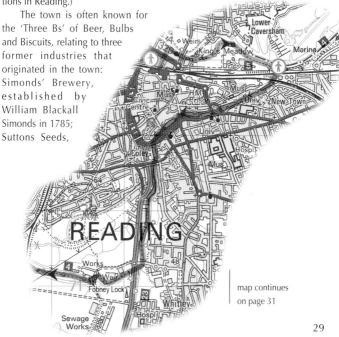

map continues
on page 31

29

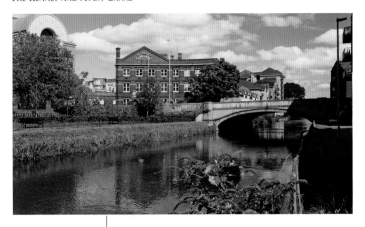

The last remaining building from the former Huntley & Palmers biscuit factory in Reading

founded in 1806 by John Sutton to provide corn seed and which expanded into flower and vegetable seeds in 1837; and Huntley & Palmers, originally started by Joseph Huntley in 1822, which by 1900 had become the largest biscuit manufacturer in the world.

The journey of 152.1km (94½ miles) along the Kennet and Avon Canal starts at Kennet Mouth, where the canal and River Kennet join with England's longest river, the Thames.

The Thames rises in Gloucestershire and meanders for 346km (215 miles) through eight counties. The 72km (45 mile) **River Kennet** rises at several locations, including Swallowhead Spring close to Silbury Hill

(Avebury), and meets up with the canal on numerous occasions throughout the first two stages.

Head away from the River Thames (canal on right), passing under two railway bridges. Pass the Jolly Anglers pub (0118 376 7823), Blake's Lock and the Fisherman's Cottage pub (0118 956 0432), following Kennet Side. ▶

Pass under two road bridges and ignore a footbridge, joining Duke's Street beside a bridge. Cross slightly left and keep ahead, following the left-hand side of the canal through the Oracle Shopping Centre. ▶

At Bridge Street, cross over the canal to follow the right-hand side of the combined canal and river past the weir, with County Lock (106) over to the left. (The brick building on the right, now a restaurant, was once part of the Simonds' Brewery.) Continue for 2.7km, passing under four bridges, keeping close to the canal. At Fobney Lock (105), follow the path past some buildings, then swing left across a bridge and turn right past the lock; a gate on the left gives access to Fobney Island Wetland Nature Reserve.

There are 105 locks to pass, from Blake's Lock (107) to Bristol's Hanham Lock (1). Lock 98 is disused, and locks 8 and 9 have been combined.

This was the site of the former Simonds' Brewery (demolished in 1983) and the narrow section of canal was known as the 'Brewery Gut'.

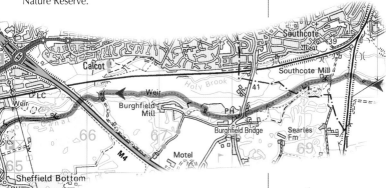

Leave Fobney Island via the bridge over the **weir** and turn right to continue alongside the canal, soon passing under the railway bridge. Turn right over the footbridge and go left, ignoring a footbridge (12) on the right, and pass

map continues on page 33

Garston Lock is one of only two turf-sided locks along the canal; the other is Monkey Marsh Lock (Stage 2)

Southcote Lock (104). Keep ahead for 1.3km to reach Burghfield Bridge (14); here, on the left, is the thatch-roofed Cunning Man pub (0118 959 8067).

Keep ahead and cross over the canal at the next foot-bridge (15), before continuing past Burghfield Lock (103). Cross a stile and continue through a large open field to a path junction on the far side near a pillbox (this is the first of many to be seen along the canal – see 'Brief history of the canal' in the Introduction). Turn left over Hissey's Bridge (17) and then turn right, soon passing under the **M4** to reach Garston Lock (102), beside two pillboxes.

Continue along the canal past the lock (101), passing a sign that says it is 6 miles back to Reading and 13½ miles to Newbury (and a car park on the left, SU 648 705), to reach the road and bridge (19) to the south of **Theale**. Some 650 metres to the left along the road is the Fox and Hounds (0118 930 2295) at **Sheffield Bottom**; 550 metres to the right is the railway station, with Theale village 400 metres further on (pubs, shops, post office and accommodation).

Along the main street in **Theale** are a number of interesting buildings including the late 15th-century thatch-roofed Old Lamb Hotel (0118 930 2357). The more recent Victorian Gothic-style Holy Trinity Church, inspired by Salisbury Cathedral, is built of Bath stone that was brought along the canal in the 1830s. The village has four pubs: the Bull (0118 930 3478), the Crown Inn (0118 930 2310), the Volunteer (0118 930 2489) and the Falcon (0118 930 2523). The railway line, originally opened in the 1840s, now forms the line from London to the south-west and closely follows the canal as far as Pewsey (Stage 3).

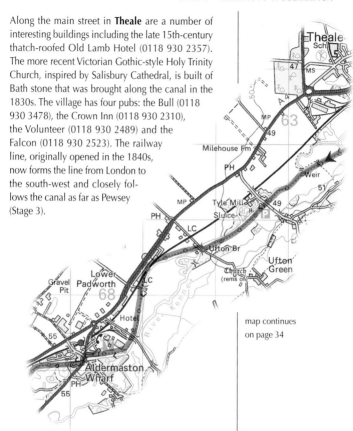

map continues
on page 34

Keep ahead alongside the canal, passing a flooded gravel pit, then a lock (100) followed by a swing bridge. The route then follows a meandering river section through a field to reach a minor road bridge (23) at **Tyle Mill**, where there is parking (SU 626 691). ▶

Continue along the south side of the canal, past Tyle Mill Lock (99) and soon passing through open fields. At **Ufton Bridge** turn right across the River Kennet and the

Some 500 metres north-west, at the junction with the A4, is the Spring Inn pub (0118 930 3440); 800 metres south-east is Sulhamstead (accommodation).

For the railway station, turn right along the A340 then fork left along Station Road (200 metres each way); 200 metres to the left is the Butt Inn (0118 971 3309, accommodation).

canal before immediately turning left to rejoin the towpath beside the disused Ufton Lock (98); the canal and River Kennet are now separate for 4.3km.

Continue along the right-hand side of the canal for 2.5km, passing two bridges (26 and 27) and two locks (97 and 96) to reach the A340 and lift bridge (28) at **Aldermaston Wharf**. On the right, shortly before the main road, is the canal visitor centre and tea room (0118 971 2868), housed in a former canal worker's cottage. ◄

> **Aldermaston Wharf** dates from the 1720s, when the River Kennet between Reading and Newbury was made navigable (the Kennet Navigation). Aldermaston Lock was once known as Brewhouse Lock because the Aldermaston Brewery – later called Strange's Brewery – was established just to the south of the lock; the buildings were demolished in the 1950s.
>
> The picturesque village of **Aldermaston** (visited in Walk 2) lies to the south-west (2.3km using the cycleway that follows the A340) and is home to the Hind's Head pub (0118 971 2194, accommodation) and shop. Just south of the village is the Atomic Weapons Establishment (AWE), which became the focus of the 'Ban the Bomb' marches in the 1950s and 60s.

The tea room and visitor centre at Aldermaston Wharf

Cross the canal via the road bridge and continue along the south side for 1.3km passing the scalloped-sided Aldermaston Lock (95). Cross the canal at Frouds Bridge (29) and after passing a meandering section, where the River Kennet rejoins the canal, cross back over via a footbridge (30). Then keep ahead to the swing bridge (31) at **Woolhampton** beside the Rowbarge pub (0118 971 2213), named after the 19th-century passenger boats that operated on the canal hereabouts. ▶

To the right is Midgham station (150 metres); further on at the A4 are village shop/tea room, post office, the Angel Inn (0118 971 3827) and bus services to Reading and Newbury.

WOOLHAMPTON

Woolhampton is in two distinct parts, with the main village, formerly a stopping-off point on the coaching route between London and Bath, strung along the A4 or Great Bath Road. On the right, where Station Road meets the A4, is a listed Victorian drinking fountain (not working) built to commemorate Queen Victoria's Diamond Jubilee (1897). To the north is Upper Woolhampton, home to the visually striking Benedictine Douai Abbey. Construction of the abbey started in 1929 in a Gothic revival style; however, work was stopped in 1933 and it was not until 1993 that the abbey was finally completed, following a much more modern style.

STAGE 2
Woolhampton to Hungerford

Start	Woolhampton Bridge (SU 572 665)
Finish	Hungerford A338 bridge (SU 338 687)
Distance	24.9km (15½ miles); cumulative 45.6km (28¼ miles)
Total ascent	180m
Time	6½hr
Map	OS Explorer 158; Heron Maps: Kennet & Avon Canal
Refreshments	Woolhampton, Midgham (A4), Thatcham, Newbury, Marsh Benham, Kintbury, Hungerford
Public transport	Railway stations at Woolhampton (Midgham station), Thatcham, Newbury, Kintbury, Hungerford; bus services at Woolhampton, Midgham (A4), Thatcham, Newbury, Kintbury, Hungerford
Accommodation	Midgham (A4), Thatcham, Newbury, Kintbury, Hungerford
Splitting the stage	The stage may be split after 10.6km (6¾ miles) at Newbury (SU 472 672), where there is a full range of facilities including a railway station.

From Woolhampton, the route continues along the Kennet Valley, meeting up with the River Kennet on several occasions and passing Thatcham – a detour gives access to the Nature Discovery Centre – to arrive at Newbury. Greenham Common, once synonymous with the Cold War, lies to the south. After passing under the A34, the route becomes more rural, passing Hamstead Park and the ideally located Dundas Arms pub overlooking the canal at picturesque Kintbury. The final stretch continues parallel with the River Kennet to end at Hungerford, close to Berkshire's western border. Along the length of the stage, the towpath passes a number of former World War II pillboxes.

From the south side of the swing bridge (31) at Woolhampton, head west between the canal and the Rowbarge pub (0118 971 2213), soon passing

map continues
on page 39

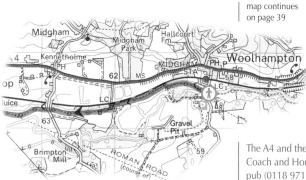

Woolhampton Lock (94). Cross over at the swing bridge (33), pass a lock (93) and cross back again at the next swing bridge (35).

Continue along the south side for 3.3km, passing under the minor road at Midgham Bridge (36). ▸ After passing Midgham Lock (92), keep ahead to pass a bridge, then a row of houses and then Colthrop Lock (91) to reach the road bridge (42) at **Thatcham**. ▸

Thatcham, which offers a full range of services, has a long history stretching back several millennia and it was here that the Roman road between Calleva

The A4 and the Coach and Horses pub (0118 971 3384) are 500 metres to the north; the Berkshire Arms (0118 971 4114, accommodation) is 400 metres west along the A4.

To the right is Thatcham railway station, with the Swan pub (01635 862084, accommodation) 75 metres further on.

The Rowbarge pub at Woolhampton marks the end of Stage 1 and the start of Stage 2

Atrebatum (Silchester) and Corinium (Cirencester) crossed the River Kennet. Just to the east of the town, on the north side of the canal, was the location of Colthrop Mill (closed in 2000), where paper had been produced for over 200 years.

Cross the canal at the bridge and continue along the north side past **Monkey Marsh Lock** (90); this is the second of only two turf-sided locks on the canal (the first – Garston Lock – was passed in Stage 1) and dates from the opening of the Kennet Navigation around 1720. Continue along the north side of the canal for 3.9km, passing Widmead Lock (89).

The path to the right, just after the lock, leads across the railway (care required) to the **Nature Discovery Centre**. The wildlife centre, managed by Berks, Bucks & Oxon Wildlife Trust (BBOWT), consists of several flooded gravel pits that provide a habitat for a wide variety of wildlife including damselflies, dragonflies, common terns, and plants such as purple loosestrife and yellow flag iris; the area is also a good place to see a range of wintering wildfowl. The adjacent **Thatcham Reedbeds** reserve, one

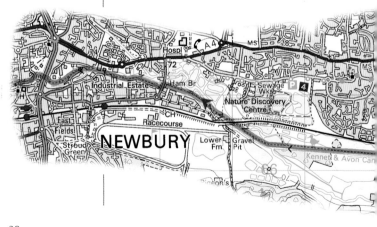

of the largest areas of inland reedbed in southern England, is home to warblers (reed, sedge and Cetti's) and the diminutive Desmoulin's snail. The centre has a café and toilets (800 metres each way).

The Teashop by the Canal and restored wharfside crane at Newbury

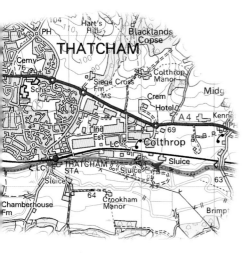

map continues on page 43

39

Head under a railway bridge and then past Bull's Lock (88) and a swing bridge to reach **Ham Bridge** (B3421). Cross to the south side of the canal and continue past Ham Lock (87) before crossing back to the north side at bridge 53. Continue over a footbridge at the boatyard (marina) entrance and then pass a lock (86). Keep ahead past a footbridge and soon, across the canal on the left, is Newbury Marina.

Pass under the A339 and continue, with Victoria Park on the right; the next bridge (59) gives access to Newbury Wharf and **Newbury** town centre (full range of facilities).

NEWBURY

To access the town centre, bear right just before the bridge (59), then turn sharp left to head south across the canal to an area that used to be Newbury Wharf; over to the left is a small stone building housing the Teashop by the Canal (01635 522609), while to the right are toilets. Newbury Wharf marked the terminus of the Kennet Navigation until the Kennet and Avon Canal was completed.

Keep ahead for 75 metres and turn right along Wharf Street alongside the 17th-century Granary (former grain store) and Cloth Hall, which now houses the West Berkshire Museum (01635 519562), to reach the Market Place (market days are Thursday and Saturday). Straight on leads to Bartholomew Street and St Nicolas' Church (keep ahead and you soon rejoin the canal at West Mills). To access the railway station, head south through the Market Place, then follow Cheap Street for 300 metres, later curving right to the station.

In the late 15th century, Newbury was highly regarded for its cloth and the town's most famous clothier was John Smallwood (or Winchcombe), known as 'Jack of Newbury'. He helped fund the rebuilding of St Nicolas' Church (visited in Walk 4), a fine example of an early 16th-century Perpendicular-style 'wool church'; the church contains a memorial to him.

To the south-east of the town is Newbury Racecourse, which opened in 1905, and Greenham Common (visited in Walk 3), a name synonymous with women's peace camps during the Cold War. The airbase has now gone and much of the land has been reverted to open common, home to a wide variety of wildlife.

Continue along the north side of the canal towards Town Bridge (60). Go straight across the pedestrianised street heading towards the Lock, Stock and Barrel pub (01635 580550), bear left through the alleyway to the canal and turn right along the towpath over Lock Island passing Newbury Lock (85). ▶

Cross the canal at the swing bridge (62) to join West Mills road and turn right between the cottages and the canal. Follow the south side of the canal for 1.3km, heading towards open countryside, before crossing over via the bridge (64) just before Guyer's Lock (84). On the way, across the canal, is the brick abutment of a bridge that carried the Lambourn Valley Railway over the canal; the line, which opened in 1898, finally closed in 1973.

Continue for 7.2km, passing under the **A34**, then passing a lock (83) and the railway bridge (65), then another bridge (66) and lock (82) to reach a minor road bridge beside a pillbox, with **Marsh Benham** to the right. ▶

Hamstead Marshall originally developed close to the banks of the River Kennet and this is where the

Wire Lock (76) between Kintbury and Hungerford

To the right is a granite sculpture called Ebb and Flow, by Peter Randall-Page, which fills and empties with the movement of water through the lock.

For the Red House pub (01635 582017), turn right along the road to the crossroads and go right (600 metres each way); left leads to Hamstead Marshall.

41

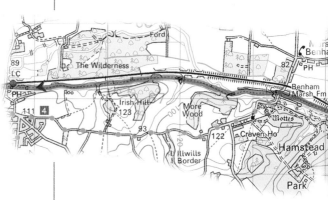

12th-century St Mary's Church is located. In 1661, the 1st Earl of Craven commissioned the Dutch architect Sir Balthazar Gerbier to build a grand mansion in **Hamstead Park**. Unfortunately the house was extensively damaged by fire in 1718 and was later demolished; all that remain today are several pairs of elaborate gateposts just south of the church (visited on Walk 5). A quick look at the map reveals that there are three earth mounds near the church that were built as motte-and-bailey castles during the late 11th or early 12th century.

On the opposite bank, after Dreweat's Lock, is Irish Hill, the site of an old whiting works, where chalk was ground into a fine powder for use in products such as paint.

After crossing the road, continue straight on past three more locks: Hamstead (81), Copse (80) and Dreweat's (79). ◀ Keep ahead past Shepherd's Bridge (73) to arrive at the road bridge (75) at **Kintbury**. Just to the right is the railway station, across the road is parking and toilets, and to the left is the perfectly located canalside Dundas Arms pub (01488 658263, accommodation).

Kintbury is home to the picturesque 12th-century St Mary's Church, which houses several interesting monuments. To visit the church, either turn left along the road for 400 metres or turn left at the

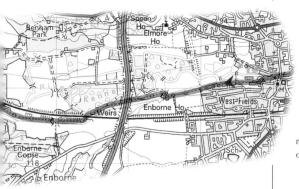

map continues
on page 45

next bridge (76) and follow the path up past the Old Vicarage. A local legend tells of the Kintbury Great Bell, which once hung in the church tower; when the tower was destroyed by a great storm, the bell supposedly sank into the River Kennet and has remained hidden there ever since, despite many attempts to retrieve it.

There is also a shop and post office, the Blue Ball pub (01488 608126) and the Cocochoux Cake Café (01488 658717).

Continue along the north side of the canal for 3.7km, passing three locks (78, 77 and 76) and five bridges. After the first bridge (76), look left for a view of the 19th-century Old Vicarage, with the church tower behind. An earlier vicarage stood on the same site and was visited on a number of occasions by the great romantic novelist Jane Austen.

The River Kennet is quite close at times, on the right, as the canal approaches a minor road at Dunmill Bridge (82); this is the last time that we see the River Kennet – the canal now follows the River Dun towards Crofton. A short way to the left along the road is a car park (SU 351 681). ▶

Some 100 metres to the right, past a pillbox, is the picturesque Denford Mill, once used as a fulling mill, where rough woven cloth was cleaned and thickened (now a private house).

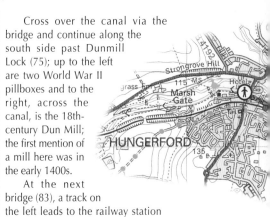

Cross over the canal via the bridge and continue along the south side past Dunmill Lock (75); up to the left are two World War II pillboxes and to the right, across the canal, is the 18th-century Dun Mill; the first mention of a mill here was in the early 1400s.

At the next bridge (83), a track on the left leads to the railway station (100 metres). The route keeps ahead to reach the old wharf just after passing under the A338 (bridge 84) in **Hungerford**; for the main street, turn left.

Across the canal, near Hungerford, stands 18th-century Dun Mill

44

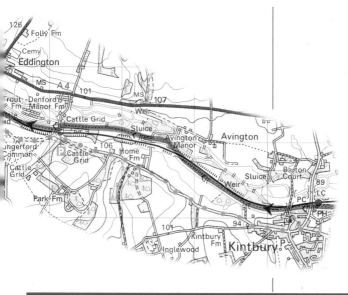

HUNGERFORD

The market town of Hungerford, the name of which is derived from a Saxon word meaning 'hanging wood ford', lies close to the western edge of Berkshire. The town is the only place in the country that still holds the Hocktide Festival, which relates to the rights of the commoners; the highlight is Tutti Day (second Tuesday after Easter), when the Hocktide Court is held and the Tutti Men visit every house with common rights. The present St Lawrence's Church (passed in Stage 3), built from Bath stone transported along the canal, dates from 1816; inside is the much mutilated effigy of Sir Robert de Hungerford (d.1352).

About 200 metres north along the A338, at the junction with the A4, is the Bear Hotel. It was here, in 1688 during the 'Glorious Revolution', that William of Orange stayed on his way from Devon to London, having been invited to 'invade' England by Protestant nobles who were disenchanted with the rule of the Catholic King James II. Days later, James II fled to France, opening the way for William to rule jointly as William III with Mary II; a plaque on the wall commemorates the historic event.

STAGE 3
Hungerford to Pewsey Wharf

Start	Hungerford A338 bridge (SU 338 687)
Finish	Pewsey Wharf (SU 157 610)
Distance	22.8km (14¼ miles); cumulative 68.4km (42½ miles)
Total ascent	150m
Time	6hr
Map	OS Explorer 157 and 158; Heron Maps: Kennet & Avon Canal
Refreshments	Hungerford, Froxfield, Great Bedwyn, Crofton, Wilton, Stibb Green, Wootton Rivers, Easton Royal, Pewsey Wharf, Pewsey
Public transport	Railway stations at Hungerford, Great Bedwyn, Pewsey; bus services at Hungerford, Froxfield, Great Bedwyn, Pewsey Wharf, Pewsey
Accommodation	Hungerford, Froxfield, Crofton, Wolfhall, Wootton Rivers, Easton Royal, Pewsey
Splitting the stage	The stage may be split after 7.9km (5 miles) at Great Bedwyn (SU 280 644), where there is a railway station and parking.

Stage 3 leaves behind West Berkshire and heads into Wiltshire. For most of this section, as in the previous two stages, the canal is followed by the railway, which opened in 1862 and now forms the line from London to the south-west. After passing through historic Great Bedwyn, the canal arrives at Crofton Pumping Station and Beam Engines, home to the oldest working steam-driven beam engine in the world. The canal then heads for the Vale of Pewsey, described by William Cobbett in his *Rural Rides* (where it is known as 'Valley of Avon' – this is where the Hampshire River Avon rises) as his 'land of promise' and 'a most beautiful sight'.

From Hungerford (see Stage 2), the towpath follows the south (left) side of the canal for 7.9km to Great Bedwyn, passing **Hungerford Lock** (74) and then **St Lawrence's**

Church beside the swing bridge (85). Continue straight on along the towpath, passing through gates, to enter a field that forms part of Freeman's Marsh, then keep ahead to reach **Hungerford Marsh Lock** (73) with its central swing bridge (86).

map continues on page 49

Since the 14th century, registered commoners have had the right to fish and graze animals on **Freeman's Marsh** and these rights are still exercised under the rules of the Hocktide Court. More importantly, the marsh supports a rich wildlife: marsh marigolds and southern marsh orchids grow in the wet meadows, while the River Dun, a typical chalk stream, is home to trout and bullheads, plants such as yellow iris and water crowfoot, and the endangered water vole; birds include kingfishers and reed buntings.

To visit **Cobbs Farm Shop & Kitchen** (01488 686770), cross the canal via the swing bridge (86) and turn left towards the house. Bear right along the track, cross the footbridge over the River Dun and go through a gate to reach the A4, with the shop opposite; retrace your steps back to the canal (650 metres each way).

Some 400 metres further on are the late 17th-century almshouses. Originally built to house widows of clergymen, the quadrangle of 50 cottages still provides sheltered housing for women.

Continue straight on to pass Cobblers Lock (72) and a footbridge, then go under the railway bridge and past a lock (71) to reach a minor road bridge (90); from here, a short detour (350 metres each way) to the right along the minor road then left beside the A4 leads to the Pelican Inn (01488 682479, accommodation) at **Froxfield**. ◀

The route now leaves Berkshire and continues through Wiltshire, passing three locks (parking at lock 68, SU 299 671) and two bridges to reach lock 67 at **Little Bedwyn**; just before the lock, the footbridge (93) across the canal and railway gives access to St Michael's Church.

St Michael's Church, just off the canal at Little Bedwyn

Little Bedwyn, a small village straddling the River Dun, canal and railway, was known as Estbedwinda in 1177. It is home to St Michael's Church, dating from the 12th century, some picturesque cottages and an upmarket restaurant, the Harrow. A short way to the west is Chisbury and the remains of an Iron Age hill fort. Within the earthworks, near Chisbury Manor Farm, is the empty shell of St Martin's Chapel (English Heritage), which dates from the 13th century.

Keep ahead under the road bridge and pass a further two locks to reach the road bridge (95) at **Great Bedwyn**.

Great Bedwyn has a railway station, shop, post office and two pubs: the Three Tuns (01672 870280) and the Cross Keys (01672 870332). It also has a rather large church, the Church of St Mary the Virgin, which dates from 1092 although most of what is visible dates from the 12th and 13th centuries. Step inside to see an impressive monument to Sir John Seymour, father of Jane Seymour who married King Henry VIII in 1536, becoming his third wife; their son became Edward VI. The church also holds the stone figure of a knight, believed to be Sir Adam de Stokke (d.1313), and the tomb of Sir Roger de Stokke (d.1333), son of Sir Adam.

Continue under the road bridge, past the parking area (SU 280 644), and continue along the south side of the canal for 2.9km, passing four locks to reach lock 60, with **Crofton Pumping Station**

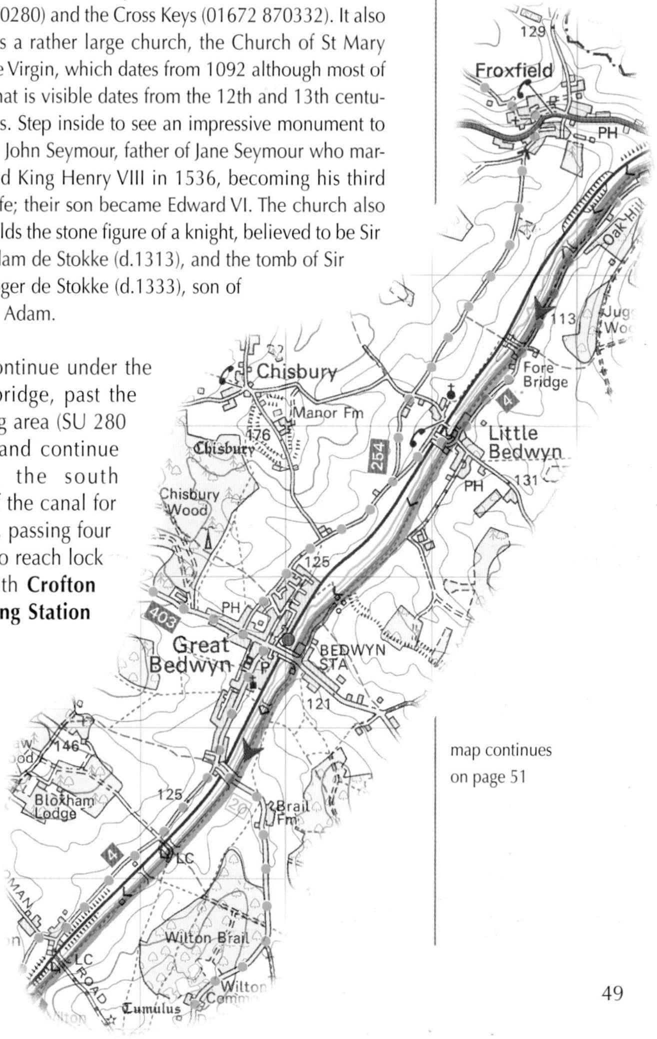

map continues
on page 51

49

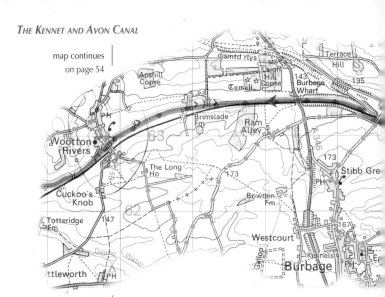

map continues
on page 54

At lock 61, a crossing track follows the course of a Roman road that ran between Venta Bulgarum (Winchester) and Cunetio (near Mildenhall).

and Beam Engines on the right and **Wilton Water** on the left; a waymarked path heads south-east alongside Wilton Water to reach the Swan (01672 870274) at Wilton (1km each way). ◄

Just east of Wilton village is **Wilton Windmill**. Originally built in 1821, it has been lovingly restored to full working condition and is Wiltshire's only working windmill. The fantail keeps the sails aligned with the wind, acting as an automatic rudder (01672 870266).

To visit Crofton Pumping Station and Beam Engines
Cross the canal via the lock gate and follow the path through the tunnel under the railway, then up the steps; retrace your steps back across the canal and turn right.

The world-famous **Crofton Pumping Station** was built in 1807 so that water from natural springs at Wilton could be raised by 12m to the summit of the canal to replenish the water lost each time a boat

50

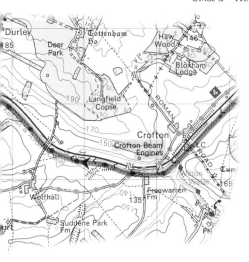

went through a lock. Wilton Water, on the opposite bank, was created in 1836 to provide a larger store of water that could be pumped into the canal. Although electric pumps are now used to pump water into the canal, Crofton's magnificent steam-driven beam engines – one of which is the oldest working beam engine in the world – are still used on several occasions throughout the year (01672 870300).

The route continues along the south side of the canal, passing five locks and the brick abutments of the former railway bridges of the Swindon, Marlborough and Andover Railway. After passing Crofton Top Lock (55), the route is following the highest section – the summit pound – of the canal, which stretches for 4km to Cadley Lock (54).

At Wolfhall Bridge (103), a track heads south for 600 metres to **Wolfhall**. Suddene Park Farm, which offers B&B and a campsite, is 500 metres further on.

Wolfhall was once the home of Sir John and Lady Margaret Seymour. Their daughter Jane married

Henry VIII as his third queen and gave him a son (Edward VI); Henry VIII visited in 1535 and 1539. The great manor has long since disappeared; the present Wolfhall Manor is Victorian. The house gave its name to Hilary Mantel's novel *Wolf Hall*.

Just to the left is the former Savernake Forest Hotel, built in 1864 (now private houses).

Shortly before the entrance to the Bruce Tunnel, fork up to the left (or turn up the steps at the tunnel entrance and then turn right) and keep ahead to cross the minor road. ◀

The 459-metre-long **Bruce Tunnel** (the only long tunnel on the canal) is named after the local land-owner, Thomas Brudenell-Bruce, Earl of Ailesbury, who lived at nearby Tottenham House. The tunnel has no towpath, which meant that the horse-drawn barges had to be pulled through the tunnel by the boatmen using chains fixed to the walls, while the horses were taken over the top.

The plaque at the Bruce Tunnel commemorates a local landowner, Thomas Brudenell-Bruce, Earl of Ailesbury

Continue along the enclosed path, soon heading down steps to pass under the railway, and then bear left along the south side of the canal to pass **Burbage Wharf** just after passing under the A346 bridge (104).

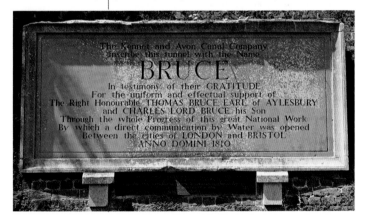

At **Burbage Wharf**, on the opposite bank, is a replica wharfside crane (private). These were once a common sight along the canal. Just to the north is Savernake Forest, a tranquil remnant of a much larger medieval royal hunting ground, first mentioned in a Saxon charter dated AD934. William the Conqueror gave Savernake to one of his knights, and it has passed in an unbroken line for over 30 generations. Although privately owned, it has been leased to the Forestry Commission and walkers can explore large parts of the forest.

To the south there is a pub at Stibb Green (Three Horseshoes, 01672 810324) and at Burbage there is a pub (White Hart, 01672 810336) and shop.

After Cadley Lock (54) and bridge, the canal heads downhill all the way to Bristol and the water that passes through each lock now drains towards the River Avon; prior to this point the water drains towards the River Thames. Continue past a further two locks with bridges to reach another lock (51) and the road bridge (108) at **Wootton Rivers**. ▶

Burbage Wharf is home to a replica wharfside crane

Some 375 metres north along the road is the thatch-roofed Royal Oak pub (01672 810322, accommodation); 1.9km south at Easton Royal is the Bruce Arms pub and campsite (01672 810216).

53

First recorded in AD804, **Wootton Rivers** gained part of its name from the de la Rivière family, who held the manor from the early 13th century. In the mid 15th century, the manor was sold to Sir John Seymour of Savernake and then passed through a succession of Seymours and Dukes of Somerset until it was bequeathed to St John's College, Cambridge, in 1692.

St Andrew's Church, which dates from the 14th century, has a picturesque wooden steeple and a clock made in 1911 by local man John Spratt to commemorate George V's coronation. On one face of the clock, the numbers have been replaced with the words 'Glory be to God'.

The White Horse Trail crosses here, leading to Pewsey. To visit, head south along the track and along Hollybush Lane; at the mini-roundabout, turn right along the B3087 to the Market Place (1.5km each way).

The route now follows the longest pound (section between neighbouring locks) of the canal, stretching for 24km (15 miles), so there are no locks all the way to Devizes (Stage 4).

Cross the road and continue along the south side for 4km to reach the fifth bridge (Pains Bridge, 113). Here a gate on the left gives access to Jones's Mill Nature Reserve (Wiltshire Wildlife Trust). ◄

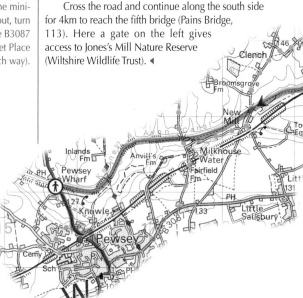

54

Jones's Mill was previously used as a traditional water meadow that was allowed to flood with mineral-rich spring-fed waters during the winter to produce an early growth of grass in the spring. Plants such as yellow iris and great horsetail thrive here as well as rarer plants including bog pimpernel.

To complete the stage, keep ahead for 800 metres to arrive at **Pewsey Wharf** and the A345. Here there is a car park, bus stop for services between Salisbury and Swindon (except Sundays), and a pub: the Waterfront (01672 564020).

For Pewsey village and railway station
To reach the railway station, turn left following the road (pavement) for 800 metres; before the railway bridge, fork right to the station. For the village, keep ahead along the road for 25 metres and just before the railway bridge turn left along Ways Way for 100 metres. Then turn right along Buckleaze Lane to the A345 and bear left along the A345 for 400 metres to the Market Place (this avoids the narrow section on the A345 under the railway bridge where there is no pavement).

PEWSEY

The history of Pewsey can be traced back to Saxon times, when it was held by Alfred the Great, who became King of Wessex in AD870; in 1913, a statue of Alfred was unveiled in the Market Place to commemorate the Coronation of King George V. In AD940, Alfred's grandson Edmund granted the royal estate to St Peter's Abbey in Winchester (later Hyde Abbey) and they held the manor until Henry VIII's Dissolution of the Monasteries.

The village has a number of interesting buildings, including the thatched and cruck-framed Ball House, located on Ball Corner, which dates back to the 14th century. Others include Bridge Cottage on the High Street and the Court House beside the Church of St John the Baptist; the church dates back to Norman times. Just off the High Street, part of the old iron foundry, established by George Whatley, is now home to the Pewsey Heritage Centre (01672 562617), which houses an interesting collection of artefacts covering life in the village over the last two centuries.

STAGE 4
Pewsey Wharf to Devizes

Start	Pewsey Wharf (SU 157 610)
Finish	Devizes Wharf (SU 005 618)
Distance	19.3km (12 miles); cumulative 87.7km (54½ miles)
Total ascent	160m
Time	5hr
Map	OS Explorer 157; Heron Maps: Kennet & Avon Canal
Refreshments	Pewsey Wharf, Pewsey, Wilcot, Honeystreet, All Cannings, Bishops Cannings, Horton Bridge, Coate, Devizes
Public transport	Railway station at Pewsey; bus services at Pewsey Wharf, Pewsey, Bishops Cannings, Devizes
Accommodation	Pewsey, Wilcot, Honeystreet, All Cannings, Coate, Devizes
Splitting the stage	The stage may be split after 9.5km (6 miles) at All Cannings Bridge (SU 076 622), where there is parking.

From Pewsey Wharf, the canal continues to meander through the beautiful Vale of Pewsey, following the longest pound (area between two locks) along the canal, stretching for 24km from Wootton Rivers (Stage 3) to Devizes. At Woodborough Bridge, a short detour up Woodborough Hill rewards you with a great panoramic view across the vale. Other short detours en route to Devizes take you to picturesque villages, some with pubs and accommodation.

From Pewsey Wharf (see Stage 3 for facilities), go under the A345 bridge and follow the south side of the canal. Cross over at the next bridge (115) and continue along the north side, soon passing the **Stowell Park Suspension Bridge** (116), designed by James Dredge in 1845, to reach a bridge at **Wilcot**. Here, a 300-metre detour to the left along the road leads to the Golden Swan pub (01672 562289), which has accommodation and a campsite.

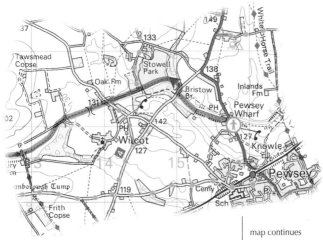

map continues
on page 59

Continue, passing Bowden's Bridge, Wide Water and then Lady's Bridge (120), where to appease the local landowner (Lady Susannah Wroughton) a more elaborate stone bridge with balustrade was built and the canal was widened to form a more landscaped lake setting. The track to the left leads to the **Swanborough Tump** on the south side of the road (500 metres each way), where in AD871 Alfred the Great met his elder brother, King Ethelred I, on their way to fight the invading Danes.

Continue along the north side – the **White Horse Trail** follows the canal for a while – to Woodborough Bridge (122). From here it's worth taking a short detour up **Woodborough Hill** for an extensive view with Salisbury Plain to the south and the Pewsey Downs, including the Alton Barnes White Horse, to the north. To visit, head northwards along the track, pass some barns and later go through a gate and climb more steeply to the top of the hill, passing some trees (800 metres each way); retrace your steps back to the canal.

Cross over the canal and follow the south side past a bridge to reach the road bridge (124) at **Honeystreet**,

▸ High up on the downs is the Alton Barnes White Horse hill figure, commissioned by Robert Pile in 1812.

map continues on page 61

with the neighbouring villages of Alton Barnes and Alton Priors a short walk away along the minor road (1km each way). ◂

Honeystreet is home to a café (01672 851232), accommodation and a pub with adjoining campsite (see the Barge Inn below). Some 300 metres north along the road is a field entrance on the left, giving access to a memorial on the last remaining air-raid shelter (SU 104 617) from the World War II RAF Alton Barnes, which was located in these fields.

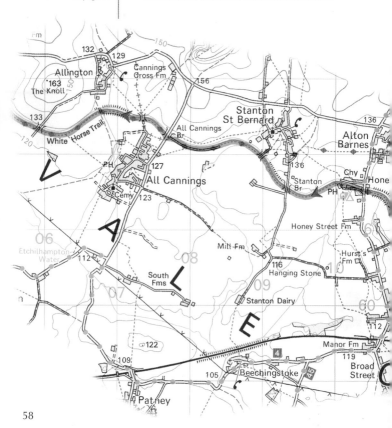

Dating back to Saxon times, the Church of St Mary the Virgin in **Alton Barnes** contains some interesting monuments, a Georgian gallery and a fine 16th-century tie-beamed and wind-braced roof.

All Saints Church in the neighbouring village of **Alton Priors** dates from Norman times. Now cared for by the Churches Conservation Trust, the church contains a tomb chest to William Button

The Alton Barnes White Horse can be seen to the north from the canal at Honeystreet

59

(d.1590), some fine Jacobean carved wooden choir stalls, and two sarsen stones hidden under trapdoors in the floor. These stones may be from an earlier sacred site, since early Christian churches were sometimes built on existing religious sites. Outside in the churchyard stands an ancient yew tree (another pagan symbol), said to be well over a thousand years old.

Continue under the bridge and after 300 metres pass the Barge Inn and campsite (01672 851705). Keep ahead for 2.8km (the next two bridges give access to **Stanton St Bernard**) to arrive at a third bridge **All Cannings Bridge** (127), where there is parking (SU 076 622).

Keep ahead under the bridge for 400 metres to another bridge, Woodway Bridge (128). From here, a detour (900 metres each way) to the left leads to **All Cannings**, home to a shop, the King's Arms pub (01380 860328) and the 13th-century All Saints Church.

The towpath passes the Barge Inn at Honeystreet

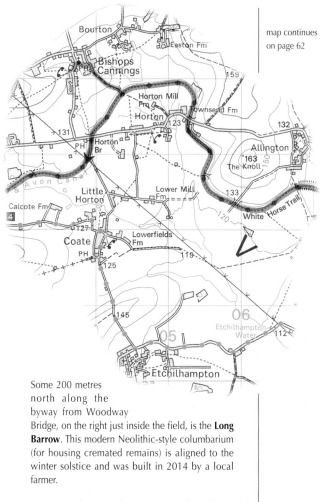

map continues
on page 62

Some 200 metres north along the byway from Woodway Bridge, on the right just inside the field, is the **Long Barrow**. This modern Neolithic-style columbarium (for housing cremated remains) is aligned to the winter solstice and was built in 2014 by a local farmer.

From Woodway Bridge, continue along the south side of the canal for 4.5km, passing three bridges (plus a disused swing bridge), to arrive at a swing bridge (133); from here, a detour (800 metres each way) leads to

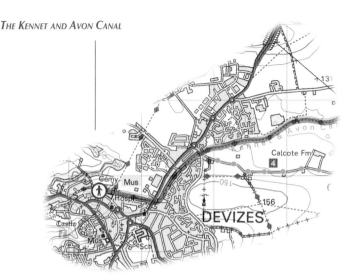

Bishops Cannings, where there is a pub and an interesting church (1.5km further south is a campsite).

Detour to Bishops Cannings
Cross the canal via the swing bridge (133) and take the left-hand fork (track) heading north-west. Keep ahead along the street for 75 metres and turn left along Church Walk past St Mary's Church, to reach the Crown Inn (01380 860218); retrace your route back to the canal.

> **St Mary's Church** dates from the mid 12th century but underwent considerable rebuilding in the 15th century and it was at this time that the impressive spire, which is clearly visible from miles around, was added. The interior of the church is well worth a visit to see the finely carved pew ends from the 1880s – each one is different – and the rare 17th-century penitent's pew. Local parishioners would sit here beneath the large painted hand – the 'hand of God' or 'hand of meditation', with warnings about vanity, mortality and sin – while they pondered their sins.

Continue for 700 metres to reach **Horton Bridge** (134); on the opposite bank is the Bridge Inn (01380 860273), while some 1.7km south is Coate and the New Inn (01380 860644, campsite). Go under the bridge and follow the towpath along the south bank of the canal, passing three bridges. From the first bridge, Laywood Bridge (135), look to the north-west for a glimpse of Wiltshire's newest chalk horse figure on Roundway Hill, created to celebrate the 2000 millennium. Further along the canal, on the opposite side, is Devizes Marina and the Hourglass pub (01380 727313); this can be accessed by a path along the north side of the canal from Laywood Bridge.

Shortly after the third bridge, the canal swings sharp right and then passes under the A361 at **Devizes**. After 550 metres, cross over New Park Road beside the bridge (139) and continue to the next bridge (140) beside Devizes Wharf; for Stage 5, cross the canal here to follow the north side. ▶

The wharf is home to the Kennet & Avon Canal Trust, a museum and café (01380 721279), and during the summer there are boat trips along the canal.

DEVIZES

The market town of Devizes offers a range of services, including a weekly Thursday market, and has a number of interesting sites.

For anyone interested in brewing, the Wadworth Brewery Visitor Centre (01380 732277) to the north-west of the Market Place is well worth a look. If you'd rather learn about Wiltshire's history over the last 6000 years, then visit the Wiltshire Heritage Museum (01380 727369), situated to the south of the Market Place. Close to the museum is St John's Church, one of two churches in the town, both of which date back to Norman times. From the churchyard you can see the present Devizes Castle (private), which was built by the Victorians on the site of a former Norman stronghold.

Some 500 metres to the east of the Market Place is the Crammer (town pond), reputedly the setting for the legend of the 'moonrakers'. Smugglers were seen by excise men trying to retrieve kegs of brandy from the pond under the light of a full moon. The quick-thinking locals said they were trying to rake in the big round of cheese, pointing to the reflection of the moon on the surface of the pond. Fortunately, the excise men went away laughing, leaving the smugglers to retrieve their brandy. Even today, many locals are proud to call themselves moonrakers.

STAGE 5
Devizes to Bradford-on-Avon

Start	Devizes Wharf (SU 005 618)
Finish	Bradford-on-Avon Lock (14) and Wharf (ST 825 602)
Distance	20.1km (12½ miles); cumulative 107.8km (67 miles)
Total ascent	100m
Time	5¼hr
Map	OS Explorer 156 and 157; Heron Maps: Kennet & Avon Canal
Refreshments	Devizes, Rowde, Sells Green, Seend, Seend Cleeve, Semington, Melksham, Hilperton Marsh, Hilperton, Trowbridge, Bradford-on-Avon
Public transport	Railway stations at Melksham, Trowbridge, Bradford-on-Avon; bus services at Devizes, Sells Green, Seend, Semington, Melksham, Hilperton Marsh, Hilperton, Trowbridge, Bradford-on-Avon
Accommodation	Devizes, Rowde, Lower Foxhangers Farm, Sells Green, Seend, Semington, Melksham, Hilperton, Trowbridge, Bradford-on-Avon
Splitting the stage	The stage may be split after 11.5km (7¼ miles) at Semington (SU 899 610), where there is parking, bus services (excluding Sundays) to railway stations at Melksham and Trowbridge, and accommodation.

From Devizes, the canal makes a dramatic descent down the world-famous Caen Hill flight of locks before passing Sells Green and then Seend; here, in Victorian times, locally quarried ironstone was smelted in three large blast furnaces. At Semington, the former Wilts & Berks Canal joined with the Kennet and Avon Canal – enthusiasts hope that one day this link will be re-established. The canal then heads to the north of Trowbridge, the county town of Wiltshire, before arriving at the southern outskirts of picturesque Bradford-on-Avon.

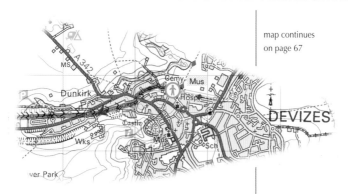

map continues
on page 67

From Devizes Wharf, cross the canal via the minor road bridge (140) and turn down to the left to follow the north side of the canal (soon, over to the left, is Wadworth's Brewery). Pass a lock (50) to join the main road (**A361**); do not cross the road but turn left across the canal and immediately turn left, then left again to head under the

Looking west down the Caen Hill flight of locks at Devizes

65

bridge (141). Follow the south side of the canal past three locks (across the canal, between locks 48 and 47, is the Black Horse pub, 01380 723930), then head under the **A361** again. Continue past two locks to reach the Sir Hugh Stockwell Lock (44), named after the former chairman of the Kennet & Avon Canal Trust, at the top of the magnificent central section of the **Caen Hill Locks** (44 through to 29). Across the bridge is the Caen Hill Café (01380 724880).

Designed by the Scottish civil engineer John Rennie (chief engineer of the Kennet and Avon Canal), the 16 locks of **Caen Hill Locks** were the last part of the canal to be completed. They form the middle group of 29 locks that cover a fall of 72m in 3.6km from Devizes to Lower Foxhangers. Due to the steepness of the terrain along the Caen Hill flight of locks (40m drop in 1km), the pounds had to be very short so they were extended sideways to allow enough water to be stored to operate each lock.

Rennie became known as one of the great canal builders in the UK, along with James Brindley, William Jessop, John Smeaton and Thomas Telford. We meet more of Rennie's work when the canal crosses the magnificent aqueducts at Avoncliff and Dundas.

map continues
on page 71

Head downhill to lock 28 and turn around for a great view back up the flight of locks before continuing under the road bridge (**B3101**). ▶ Continue past locks 27 to 23 in quick succession; the footbridge (145) on the right leads to Rowde, while to the left is Lower Foxhangers Farm (campsite and self-catering accommodation, 01380 828254).

Keep ahead and at the next bridge (146), just after the lock (22), cross the canal and continue along the north side; the solar panels on the right are used to power the Caen Hill back-pumping station that feeds water back up to the top lock on Caen Hill. Continue past the abutments of the former railway bridge (147); across the canal is **Caen Hill Marina**. The branch line from Holt Junction to Devizes was built by the Wiltshire, Somerset and Weymouth Railway and opened in 1857, with a connection to the existing line at Pewsey opening in 1862; the line through Devizes closed in 1966.

Pass under the A365 at **Martinslade** to reach a minor road bridge (149) at **Sells Green**. ▶ Keep ahead for 1.9km, passing three bridges and three locks (21 to 19). At the second bridge (151), a bridleway heads southwards, up to the junction of Rusty Lane and the A361 in **Seend** (700 metres each way). Seend village

To the left is the A361 and bus stops; 1.4km to the right along the road is Rowde, with a shop and two pubs: the Cross Keys (01380 739567) and the George and Dragon (01380 723053, accommodation).

Devizes Camping and Caravanning Club Site (01380 828839) is 100 metres to the north along Spout Lane; the Three Magpies pub (01380 828389, campsite) is 100 metres further on.

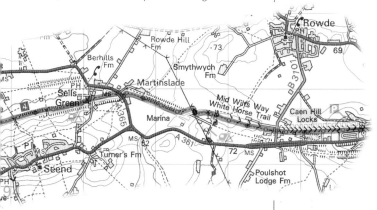

Semington Dock, where the former Wilts & Berks Canal joined the Kennet and Avon Canal

has a shop with post office, bus links to Swindon and Trowbridge, accommodation and a pub, the Bell Inn (01380 828338).

Pass under the fourth bridge (153). Just across the canal bridge, on the south side, is the Barge Inn (01380 828230); some 400 metres south along the road is the Brewery Inn (01380 828463) at **Seend Cleeve**.

The **Seend Ironworks** were located on the slope just to the south of lock 19 and consisted of three blast furnaces, where ironstone quarried from the hill above was smelted to form iron. The buildings were dismantled in the late 1880s, although quarrying continued for several decades more. A tramway was also constructed to connect the works with the branch line from Devizes (which closed in 1966). The turreted house (Ferrum House) was built as the ironmaster's residence.

Continue along the towpath for 2km, passing two locks (18 and 17) and two bridges (154 and 155), to reach a swing bridge (156) with Seend Park Farm on the left, across the canal. On the way, at bridge 155, there is a small picnic area on the right; from this bridge and the next one (156) there is a waymarked route (900 metres each way) leading to **Bowerhill** (Melksham), where there is a shop and pub (the Pilot, 01225 790599) along Blenheim Park Road.

Keep ahead to cross the aqueduct over the A350, then pass two locks (16 and 15) and Semington Dock (left) to reach **Semington Bridge** (on the right is Bridge House B&B); the former Wilts & Berks Canal joined the Kennet and Avon Canal here.

The **Wilts & Berks Canal** was completed in 1810 and ran for 84km (52 miles) from the Kennet and Avon Canal at Semington to the River Thames at Abingdon. The canal's heyday was in the 1830s, carrying materials that were to be used in the making of the Great Western Railway which, once opened, started the gradual decline in trade along the Wilts & Berks Canal until it was abandoned in 1914.

In 1977 the Wilts & Berks Canal Trust was formed. The Trust has long-term plans to open a new canal from just west of the road bridge, heading north to the River Avon at Melksham to rejoin with the original course of the canal (**www.wbct.org.uk**).

Some 400 metres to the south along the road is **Semington** and the Somerset Arms (01380 870067, accommodation). From Semington, there are bus services to Frome and Chippenham (excluding Sundays), calling at Melksham and Trowbridge.

The market town of **Melksham**, which has a range of services, lies 2.8km to the north, with the railway station a further 900 metres. Melksham's history goes back to Saxon times, when there was a ford across the River Avon, and the area was once part of a royal hunting forest. The historic quarter around Canon Square includes St Michael and All Angels Church, which dates from the 12th century.

The route continues along the north side of the canal for 8.7km to Bradford-on-Avon, soon crossing the aqueduct over the **Semington Brook**, which joins the River Avon at Whaddon. Continue past a swing bridge (161), then under two bridges and past a fourth, to reach the B3105 bridge (166) at **Hilperton Marsh**; 100 metres to the south-east along the B3105 is a shop and bus links to Trowbridge (Hilperton also has accommodation).

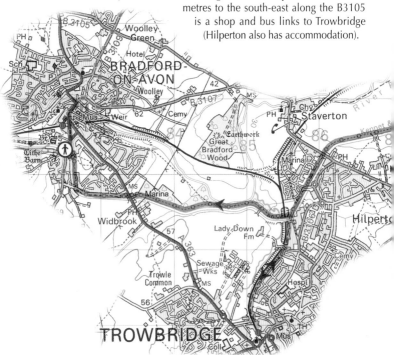

Continue under the bridge, soon crossing a bridge over the entrance to **Hilperton Marina** and then passing under a road bridge to reach bridge 168; from here a cycle path gives access to Trowbridge and the railway station.

Detour to Trowbridge

At bridge 168 (ST 855 594), turn left across the canal and then right along a path that quickly swings left and follows the railway. Keep ahead along Langford Road (houses on left) and then bear right along the surfaced path to the station (1.7km each way); the town centre is 200 metres to the left across the River Biss.

> **Trowbridge**, the county town of Wiltshire (weekly Wednesday market), was home to a Norman motte-and-bailey castle held by the de Bohun family. A stained-glass window in St James' Church depicts Henry de Bohun, who in 1215 became one of the English barons associated with King John's signing of the Magna Carta. (There is also a statue of him in the House of Lords, London.)
>
> Trowbridge became a wealthy town through the production of woollen cloth, an industry that left the town with a number of interesting buildings. To learn more about the town's history, visit Trowbridge Museum (01225 751339).

Follow the canal as it crosses the railway and River Biss via the Biss and Ladydown Aqueducts (the canal is carried here on a 9m-high embankment) and then pass Ladydown Bridge (169); shortly afterwards, down to the right through the trees, is the River Avon. Pass

The lock (14) and former wharf at Bradford-on-Avon mark the end of Stage 5

Bradford-on-Avon Marina (left) to reach the A363 road bridge (170) at **Widbrook**; 150 metres to the left along the road is the Boathouse pub (01225 309318) and bus connections to Trowbridge, Salisbury and Bath.

Continue along the canal as it swings right under a minor road bridge (171) to reach Upper Wharf and the B3109 bridge at **Bradford-on-Avon** beside lock 14. Here, there are toilets, car park, Kennet & Avon Canal Trust shop and tea room (in the former lock-keeper's cottage; 01225 868683) and during the summer there are boat trips along the canal, while on the opposite bank is the Barge Inn (01225 863403, accommodation); just across the road is the Lock Inn Café (01225 868068) and the Canal Tavern (01225 867426); off route is the railway station and town centre.

To visit Bradford-on-Avon
Turn right along the B3109 (Frome Road), passing the Canal Tavern. Keep ahead at the mini-roundabout, then

continue past the Three Horseshoes (01225 865876) to another mini-roundabout. Here, turn left for the railway station or keep ahead to reach the bridge across the River Avon; on the left, just before the bridge, is a café and tourist information centre (500 metres each way to the railway station, and a further 200 metres to the Town Bridge). For the Saxon church (St Laurence's), cross the bridge to a mini-roundabout and go left (A363) to the Swan Hotel (to the right is The Shambles), then turn left along Church Street for 200 metres.

BRADFORD-ON-AVON

The former wool town of Bradford-on-Avon – formed where the Saxons drove their carts across the 'broad ford', giving the early settlement its name – is well worth exploring, with a number of interesting buildings including the medieval Town Bridge across the River Avon. The distinctive dome-roofed lock-up was added during rebuilding of the bridge in the 17th century. On the roof of the lock-up, the weathervane in the shape of a gudgeon (type of fish) gives rise to the local saying 'under the fish and over the water'.

The timber-framed buildings in The Shambles date from Tudor times, while along Church Street is a lovely Saxon church (St Laurence's). The town's other church, the Holy Trinity, has Norman origins. To learn more about the town, visit the local museum in Bridge Street (01225 863280). (For the Tithe Barn, see Stage 6; Walk 16 explores the town's main sights.)

STAGE 6
Bradford-on-Avon to Bath

Start	Bradford-on-Avon Lock (14) and Wharf (ST 825 602)
Finish	Widcombe Lock (7), Bath (ST 753 643)
Distance	15.7km (9¾ miles); cumulative 123.5km (76¾ miles)
Total ascent	80m
Time	4hr
Map	OS Explorer 156 and 155; Heron Maps: Kennet & Avon Canal
Refreshments	Bradford-on-Avon, Avoncliff, Freshford, Limpley Stoke, Dundas, Brassknocker Basin, Monkton Combe, Bathampton, Bathford, Bath
Public transport	Railway stations at Bradford-on-Avon, Avoncliff, Freshford, Bath; bus services at Bradford-on-Avon, Limpley Stoke, Dundas, Claverton, Bathampton, Bathford, Bath
Accommodation	Bradford-on-Avon, Avoncliff, Limpley Stoke, Brassknocker Basin, Monkton Combe, Bathampton, Bathford, Bath
Splitting the stage	The stage may be split after 6.8km (4¼ miles) at Dundas (ST 783 625), where there is parking and bus services on the A36.

From Bradford-on-Avon, the canal passes through what, to many, is the most interesting and picturesque section, taking a meandering, level route through the Avon Valley and crossing the River Avon twice via the impressive Avoncliff and Dundas Aqueducts, both designed by John Rennie. Short detours off route include Bradford-on-Avon's beautiful 14th-century Tithe Barn and the Claverton Pumping Station. The stage ends at the impressive Georgian architectural gem of Bath, a great place to spend some time exploring the numerous interesting sights. While following the route, you might spot some unusual works by the artist Peter John Wells.

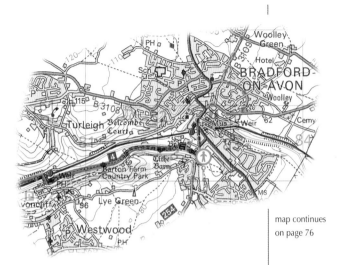

map continues
on page 76

From the B3109 bridge at Bradford-on-Avon, head westwards along the north side of the canal, passing between
the Lock Inn Café on the left (01225 868068) and Canal
Tavern on the right (01225 867426). After 250 metres,
a path on the right gives access to the impressive 14th-
century **Tithe Barn**; once owned by Shaftesbury Abbey
and used for storing food (a 'tithe' was a tenth of a tenant's produce), the 51-metre-long stone building is said
to be one of the country's finest examples of a medieval
monastic barn.

Continue along the towpath, passing the Boat Café
(barge) on the way, to reach **Avoncliff**, where the canal
swings right to arrive at the Avoncliff Aqueduct; this
impressive, late 18th-century structure built by John
Rennie takes the canal across the River Avon. ▶

For the railway
station, cross the
aqueduct with the
canal on your left
and turn right.

To follow the towpath, do not cross the aqueduct but
turn right towards the Cross Guns pub with its riverside
terrace (01225 862335, accommodation) and then sharp
left under the aqueduct, where the path splits. To continue along the canal, bear left up the steps.

The path straight on follows the River Avon to **Freshford** (1.5km each way, with a railway station and bus services to Bath and Trowbridge). The village dates back to Saxon times and the Domesday Book refers to a mill here, although Roman remains found in the area point to a much older settlement. Parts of St Peter's Church date from the 14th and 15th centuries, while the bridge and the Inn at Freshford (01225 722250) both date from the 16th century.

To visit Limpley Stoke, turn left across the river, go under the railway, then turn left along Lower Stoke for 250 metres to the Hop Pole Inn (01225 722769).

After the steps, bear left past the No. 10 Tea Gardens and then left again to cross the aqueduct with the canal on your right. Follow the south side of the canal for 4.2km, passing a bridge (174) and then going under the **B3108** bridge (175); to the left along the road is **Limpley Stoke**. ◄

map continues on page 79

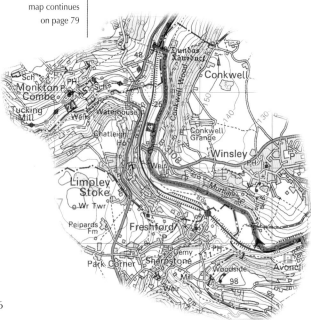

Keep ahead, with **Conkwell Wood** across the canal, and follow the towpath as it swings left to reach the **Dundas Aqueduct**.

A narrowboat crossing the impressive Avoncliff Aqueduct

Like the aqueduct at Avoncliff, the **Dundas Aqueduct** was built by John Rennie to take the canal over the River Avon. Steps down to the left just before the aqueduct give a great view of this impressive structure.

Cross the aqueduct from Wiltshire into Somerset, then cross the small bridge at the junction with the Somerset Coal Canal; 500 metres along the track to the left, just before the Somerset Coal Canal junction, is Brassknocker Basin, the Angelfish Café (01225 723483) and campsite (07970 279749). ▶

About 1km further on along the cycleway is Monkton Combe and the Wheelwrights Arms (01225 722287, accommodation).

The **Somerset Coal Canal**, which opened in 1805, joins the Kennet and Avon Canal at Dundas Wharf. It was built by the owners of several North Somerset coal mines so that they could transport their coal to Bath and Bristol. In its heyday, in the 1820s, it transported over 100,000 tons of coal a year, but competition from the railway led to its closure in 1898. Only the first 500 metres of the canal as far as Brassknocker Basin have been restored, although the Somersetshire Coal Canal Society has plans to restore more of the canal (www.coalcanal.org).

Follow the towpath to the right for 75 metres, skirting around Dundas Wharf with its cast-iron crane (the track up to the left leads to the **A36**, where there is parking, a shop at the garage, and bus services to Trowbridge and Bath). Turn right, crossing the footbridge (177) over the canal, then turn left, keeping the canal on your left for 1.8km to reach Claverton Bridge (179).

Detour to Claverton Pumping Station

Leave the canal beside the bridge, follow Ferry Lane downhill and, with care, cross the railway. **Claverton Pumping Station** is on the left. Retrace your steps back to the canal and turn right (150 metres each way).

Claverton Pumping Station was built in 1813 by the canal's chief engineer, John Rennie, to provide a better supply of water to this section of the canal. The pump, powered by a waterwheel driven by the River Avon, was used to lift water 14.5m up from the river to the canal. This remarkable piece of engineering operated for close to 140 years before falling derelict with the gradual decline of the canal. It has now been brought back to full working order by dedicated volunteers, although these days electric pumps are used to provide water to the canal. (Opening times: 01225 483001.)

Heading left (west) up Ferry Lane leads to the A36 (bus services to Bath), with Claverton village just beyond; St Mary's Church in Claverton dates from Norman times and the churchyard contains the tomb of Ralph Allen, who brought about the

map continues
on page 81

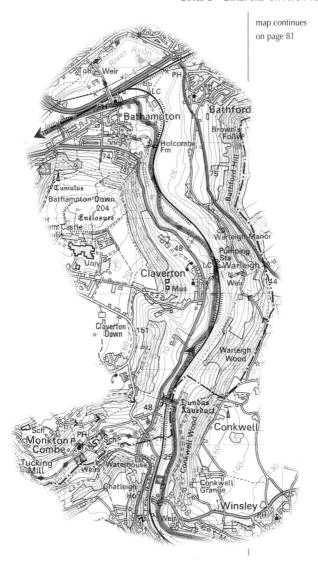

The picturesque George Inn beside the canal at Bathampton

reform of the postal service and helped in the development of Georgian Bath. Further west is early 19th-century Claverton Manor, which is now home to the American Museum in Britain (01225 460503).

Over to the right, high up on the wooded Bathford Hill, is the 19th-century Brown's Folly, built by the local Bath stone quarry owner, Wade Browne.

Continue under the bridge and pass two more bridges (181 and 182). ◄ The canal swings to the left and passes the Raft Café Boat to reach a third bridge (183) at **Bathampton**. To the left is the main part of the village with a shop and bus services, while just to the right is St Nicholas' Church. Inside the church is the Australia Chapel and the grave of Admiral Arthur Phillip, the first Governor of New South Wales, Australia.

Follow the right-hand side of the canal, passing the George Inn (01225 425079) and a row of picturesque cottages; on the opposite side of the canal once stood a plasticine factory (now demolished), opened in 1900 by art teacher William Harbutt who had invented plasticine in 1897. Pass under Candy's Bridge (184), then pass a footbridge and keep ahead through Sydney Gardens Tunnel.

Continue under two wrought-iron bridges; a gate on the right, between the two bridges, gives access to Sydney Gardens and the Holburne Museum (01225 388569), home to a café and an extensive collection of art and artefacts. Pass through Cleveland House Tunnel, double back up the path, cross the canal beside Cleveland House and then turn right, now following the left-hand side of the canal. ▶

At the next bridge (188), cross over the road and turn right across the canal, then turn sharp left down to the canal and continue along the right-hand side, passing Bath Top Lock (13); along the way, on the left, is the former Baird's Maltings building.

Continue past two more locks (beside lock 11 is the Pump Shed refreshments kiosk and an ornate chimney from the former steam pump house – see Thimble Mill below). Cross over the minor road and continue past another lock (10) to reach Bath Deep Lock (8/9); the lock was formed when the road was built over the canal by combining locks 8 and 9 to form the deepest lock along

The early 19th-century Cleveland House was the head office of the Kennet & Avon Canal Company between 1825 and 1864.

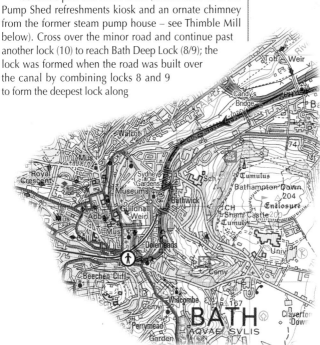

Bath Abbey has been described as England's last great Gothic church

the canal and second deepest in England, with a rise and fall of 5.7m. At the main road, turn left across the canal and immediately turn left and then left again down the steps to pass under the road. Follow the canal under another bridge, to reach **Widcombe Lock** (7), where the canal joins the Avon Navigation and the River Avon.

Across the canal, on the north bank, is the former **Thimble Mill**, built to house a steam-driven pump that raised water from the river up to lock 11, where there was another pump (passed earlier) to raise the water up to lock 13.

For the railway station, turn left to the main road (A36) and turn right for 100 metres, then go right across the footbridge over the River Avon.

Widcombe Lock marks the end of Stage 6. From here, you can detour to the centre of Bath or Bath Spa railway station. ◄

To visit Bath

From Widcombe Lock (7), turn right across the canal (bridge 194) and keep ahead with the River Avon on the left, pass under the railway bridge and follow Spring Gardens Road. Keep left, still following the river, and pass under a road bridge towards Pulteney Bridge. Go up the steps and turn left across the shop-lined bridge, built by Robert Adams in 1773. Then turn left again along Grand Parade (A3039, leading to the railway station), with the river on the left for 100 metres, before bearing right to Bath Abbey. The Roman Baths are just beyond, across the pedestrianised Abbey Churchyard. For a detailed town map see Walk 19.

BATH

The City of Bath, a World Heritage Site, offers an extensive list of interesting sights, and it would be quite easy to spend at least half a day looking around.

Bath's history stretches back more than two millennia to the Iron Age, when the hot springs here were dedicated to the goddess Sul. However, it was not until the arrival of the Romans that Bath developed into an important bathing centre, named Aquae Sulis or 'water of Sulis'. After the demise of the Roman empire, the importance of Bath's hot springs declined, until they were 'rediscovered' in the 16th century. Subsequent renovations during the Victorian era unearthed the original Roman bath complex that can be seen today.

The development of the Georgian spa town is mostly attributed to Richard 'Beau' Nash, a celebrated dandy and leader of fashion in 18th-century Britain; to Ralph Allen, onetime postmaster and owner of several Bath stone quarries; and to three architects: John Wood the Elder, who designed the elegant Circus (three curved segments of townhouses); his son, John Wood the Younger, whose most notable masterpiece is the beautiful curving Royal Crescent, built in the Palladian style; and Robert Adam, who designed the shop-lined Pulteney Bridge across the River Avon.

Adjacent to the Roman Baths is the 16th-century Bath Abbey, described as the last great Gothic church in England. The present building stands on the site of an earlier Norman abbey, which replaced an earlier Anglo-Saxon church where the first King of England, King Edgar, was crowned in AD973.

STAGE 7
Bath to Bristol

Start	Widcombe Lock (7), Bath (ST 753 643)
Finish	Neptune Statue, Floating Harbour, Bristol (ST 585 728)
Distance	28.6km (17¾ miles); cumulative 152.1km (94½ miles)
Total ascent	85m
Time	7¼hr
Map	OS Explorer 155; Heron Maps: Kennet & Avon Canal
Refreshments	Bath, Saltford, Keynsham, Hanham Mill, Conham (ferry), Crew's Hole, Bristol
Public transport	Railway stations at Bath, Keynsham, Bristol (Temple Meads); bus services at Bath, Saltford, Keynsham, Hanham Mill, Bristol
Accommodation	Bath, Saltford, Keynsham, Bristol
Splitting the stage	The stage may be split after 14.7km (9¼ miles) at Keynsham (ST 659 690), where there is a railway station and parking just off route.

The final, fairly long stage sets out from the Georgian splendour of Bath, following the Avon Navigation downstream from Widcombe Lock. After leaving Bath, the route meanders through open countryside to reach Keynsham, after which the river is hemmed in by wooded slopes as it winds its way past Conham River Park. The final section leads into the heart of Bristol, following the Feeder Canal before ending at Bristol's vibrant Floating Harbour.

Halfpenny Bridge – accessed from the A36 – leads to Bath Spa railway station; the name comes from the toll pedestrians had to pay to cross the footbridge.

From Widcombe Lock (7) – marking the junction between the canal and the Avon Navigation, which opened in 1727 – cross the minor road and follow the path ahead alongside the River Avon for 300 metres, with the A36 on the left, passing under Halfpenny (or Widcombe) Bridge; on the stonework below the footbridge are marks showing various flood levels, including the great flood of 1894. ◄ Pass under the railway bridge, then go up the

map continues
on page 87

steps, turn right across the pedestrian bridge (197)
over the river and then turn left; to the right is the bus
station.

Keep ahead across the road and after 50 metres dogleg left and continue along the riverside path heading
downstream through Green Park; the route is now following the Bristol & Bath Railway Path, a 24km (13 mile)
combined walking and cycling route between the two
cities. Pass under two road bridges to arrive at the Victoria
Suspension Bridge built in 1836 by Bath-born brewer and
engineer James Dredge, who also built the Stowell Park
Suspension Bridge (passed in Stage 4). Some 200 metres
after the bridge, a narrow path on the right leads to the
A4 beside the Hop Pole Inn (01225 446327), with the
Royal Victoria Park opposite; 200 metres west along the
A4 is the Victoria Pub & Kitchen (01225 422563) and the
Picnic in the Park café (01225 461620).

Continue under five more bridges to reach the
Weston Cut, then continue past the Dolphin Inn (01225
445048) to reach Weston Lock (6); this is the deepest
lock along the Avon Navigation. ▶ Here, the Bristol &
Bath Railway Path heads away from the River Avon, following Brassmills Lane for 500 metres before continuing
along the course of the former railway. To continue the

The digging of
the cut formed an
island, known as
'Dutch' Island after
the owner of the
early 18th-century
brass mill.

map continues
on page 93

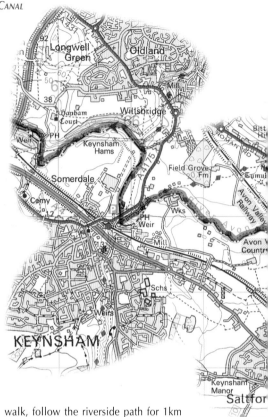

walk, follow the riverside path for 1km
(with the river on your left), passing under a
disused railway bridge (Bristol & Bath Railway
Path) and then crossing a footbridge. Pass through the
archway under the A4 beside Newbridge; ahead is the
riverside Boathouse pub (01225 482584, accommodation). Turn right up the steps and turn right again across
the River Avon; to the left is **Newbridge Park and Ride**.

Immediately after crossing the river, turn right down
the path and bear right along the track. Keep to the right
of the trees and follow the riverside path downstream
along field edges, with the River Avon on the right. After

1.4km, pass under the old railway bridge and continue as the path and river swing right, soon with Isambard Kingdom Brunel's Great Western Railway on the left (the line opened in 1841, providing a fast route between London and Bristol); the large house across the river is **Kelston Park**. ▶

Continue past Saltford Rowing Club, keeping close to the river. Cross a footbridge over the entrance to **Saltford Marina** and follow the track to the Riverside Inn (01225 873862, accommodation), with a **weir** and Kelston Lock (5) on the right (no access). As the tarmac track swings left, go straight on for a short way before turning left along the enclosed path, heading

The mid-18th-century house was built by John Wood the Younger for Sir Caesar Hawkins, Serjeant-Surgeon to Kings George II and III; Capability Brown designed the adjoining parkland.

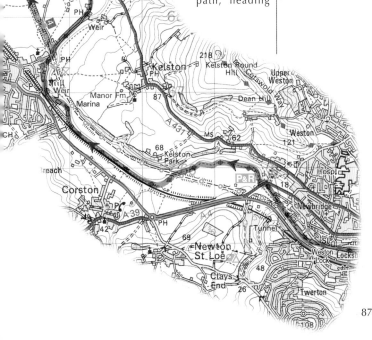

Looking across the River Avon from Saltford Lock to the former brass mill at Kelston

away from the river. Turn right along the road, soon passing Saltford Brass Mill.

Saltford Brass Mill, now a scheduled ancient monument, is the only surviving copper and brass mill built along the Avon Valley. Although closed in 1925, the mill has been fully restored and is open at certain times (0117 986 2216).

Keep ahead past a car park, picnic area and toilet (left) to reach a T-junction beside the Bird in Hand pub (01225 873335). Turn right down the road and pass under the old railway bridge. Follow the road as it swings left and then keep right at the junction, soon with the River Avon on the right.

Shortcut to Avon Riverside Station

For a shorter alternative route, fork right up the steps just before the railway bridge and turn left. Follow the Bristol & Bath Railway Path for 1.4km, rejoining the main route just after Avon Riverside Station (minus 1.7km).

At the sailing club, fork right along the enclosed path between the river and the boatyard to pass Saltford Lock

(4) and the Jolly Sailor pub (01225 873002); across the river is the former Kelston Brass Mill. Turn left through the car park and then right along the lane (the route now parts company with the river for a while). Keep ahead through a gate just to the right of the entrance to the waterworks and follow the enclosed track. Enter the field, follow the left-hand edge and leave via a gate in the top left corner. Turn right along the enclosed path back to the river and turn left, following the riverside path to Swineford Lock (3) and weir; **Swineford** is on the opposite bank (no access).

Continue, keeping the river on the right for 1.1km. Go under the railway bridge, immediately turn left along the field edge for 50 metres, then go left through a gate. Turn left along the combined path and cycleway beside the railway track; to the right is **Avon Riverside Station** (the shortcut rejoins here). Once across the bridge, fork left down the tarmac path to reach a picnic area on the north bank of the river.

The **Avon Valley Railway** (0117 932 5538) operates some steam-hauled services along part of the former branch line that ran between Bath and Mangotsfield. Most of the line, which was opened by the Midland Railway Company in 1869, now forms the Bristol & Bath Railway Path.

Turn right, cross a footbridge and follow the riverside path through six fields for 2.2km; on the opposite bank is the Avon Valley Adventure and Wildlife Park (**Avon Valley Country Park**) and then some large brick buildings (**works**) dated 1880. On the north side of the river was the site of Avon Wharf (see Londonderry Wharf below).

Exit the last field, follow the track past houses for 125 metres, then fork left along a narrow riverside path. Later, cross a footbridge over the marina entrance and continue as the river swings right to a lane in **Keynsham** beside the Lock Keeper pub (0117 986 2383), close to where the River Chew joins the River Avon. Here, a sign shows 8½ miles to Bristol and 9½ miles back to Bath. ▶

For the railway station, turn right along the lane then left along the A4175, crossing the canal and river and passing the car park. After 375 metres, the railway station is on the left.

From here, the route to Bristol follows part of the 990km (615 mile) Monarch's Way, which traces the escape route used by Charles II after his defeat by Cromwell in 1651.

Cross straight over the lane, pass under the road bridge (214) to reach Keynsham Lock (2) and continue through fields, keeping the river on the left; across the river was the site of local chocolate manufacturers, JS Fry & Sons, who built their **Somerdale** factory here following their merger with Cadbury in the 1920s (the factory closed in 2011). ◄

Keep close to the river as it swings left, then cross a bridge and pass through some gates at Londonderry Farm; this area was once the site of Londonderry Wharf.

> **Londonderry Wharf** and **Avon Wharf** (passed earlier) formed the two end stops of the Avon and Gloucestershire Railway, which opened in 1832. Known as the 'dramway', the line was built to transport coal from local mines down to boats on the river; the 'drams', or wagons, ran downhill using gravity, while the empty wagons were hauled back uphill using horses.

Follow the riverside path for 2km with Cleeve Wood up to the right, later keeping left to stay close to the river as it swings right and heads northwards to reach Ferry Road at Hanham Mill, beside the Chequers Inn (0117 329 1711). Bear left along the lane, passing the Old Lock & Weir pub (0117 967 3793). Here, the first (or in our case the last) lock on the journey along the canal – Hanham Lock – is not accessible from the north bank of the river so we have to make do with a view of the weir; below this point the river is tidal during high spring tides.

Follow the track past a row of cottages and fork left at the split, soon passing under the **A4174** bridge; the right-hand fork leads through the Avon Valley Woodlands Nature Reserve, which includes Bickley Wood, Hencliff Wood and Conham River Park. Keep along the riverside path, ignoring all routes to the right, with the railway just across the river for a time. Much of this area was quarried for pennant sandstone (see 'Geology' section in the Introduction) and the old powder house still survives below Hencliff Wood (ST 634 709).

The river heads north and then swings left. Soon, on the opposite bank, Beese's Bar and Tea Gardens (0117 977 7412), which has been here since 1846, comes into view; when open, they operate the ferry service to **Conham** across the river (ST 629 719). Follow the river as it swings right round Conham River Park, keeping left of the car park and toilets, to reach a main road.

Cross over and turn left along the pavement for 300 metres, then turn left back over the road to rejoin the riverside path (150 metres along the road is the Bull Inn, 0117 919 3028). Keep ahead for 1.8km, with houses and then some industrial buildings on the right, as the river sweeps left past **Crew's Hole**.

Crew's Hole was once an industrious place with copper mills, a tar works and a coal pit. High up on Troopers Hill – now a local nature reserve – is a tall 18th-century chimney that formed part of the copper works. To access Troopers Hill, leave the riverside path after 350 metres (ST 627 728) and turn

Beese's Bar and Tea Gardens – the owners operate the Conham Ferry during opening hours

right along the signed path between the buildings to the main road. Turn right for 50 metres, then left along Troopers Hill Road for 50 metres, passing a stone chimney stack (all that remains of the former engine house from the coal pit) and turn left to follow a path up the hill. Retrace your steps back to the river and turn right.

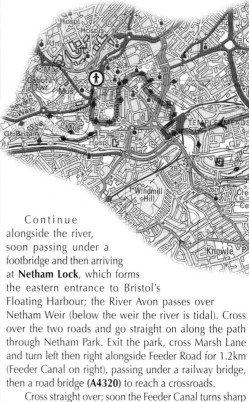

Continue alongside the river, soon passing under a footbridge and then arriving at **Netham Lock**, which forms the eastern entrance to Bristol's Floating Harbour; the River Avon passes over Netham Weir (below the weir the river is tidal). Cross over the two roads and go straight on along the path through Netham Park. Exit the park, cross Marsh Lane and turn left then right alongside Feeder Road for 1.2km (Feeder Canal on right), passing under a railway bridge, then a road bridge (**A4320**) to reach a crossroads.

Cross straight over; soon the Feeder Canal turns sharp right at Totterdown Basin, which is where the Floating Harbour takes over the course of the natural river (the

River Avon now follows the New Cut). Continue along Cattle Market Road and pass under the railway bridge to a major junction with the A4. Turn right along Temple Gate and then turn right up the entrance ramp of **Temple Meads railway station** (alternatively keep ahead and turn right along Friary Road to reach Temple Quay and turn left). ▶

Enter the station and immediately bear left, then follow the walkway (signed for Temple Quays and ferry) through the car park and past office blocks to reach the water

This area is undergoing redevelopment and the route may change (including plans for a waterside route past Totterdown Basin).

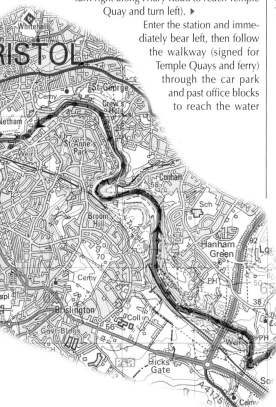

again, with a footbridge ahead (Valentine Bridge). Do not cross the bridge, but turn left, keeping the water on the right. Go under the A4044 Temple Bridge and at the next bridge

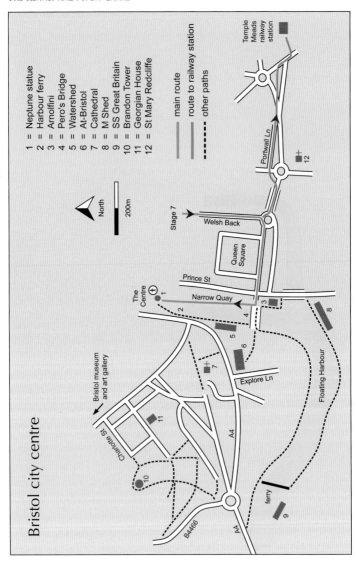

Bristol city centre

1 = Neptune statue
2 = Harbour ferry
3 = Arnolfini
4 = Pero's Bridge
5 = Watershed
6 = At-Bristol
7 = Cathedral
8 = M Shed
9 = SS Great Britain
10 = Brandon Tower
11 = Georgian House
12 = St Mary Redcliffe

North

200m

main route
route to railway station
other paths

Temple Meads railway station

Portwall Ln

12

Stage 7

Welsh Back

Queen Square

Prince St

The Centre

1

Narrow Quay

2

3

5

6

4

8

7

Explore Ln

Bristol museum and art gallery

11

Chandle St

A4

Floating Harbour

10

B4466

A4

ferry

9

(St Philip's Bridge), leave the waterside path and cross over the road.

The unusual 43m-high **concrete tower** across the water was built in 1969 for the manufacture of lead shot. Molten lead was poured through a sieve and allowed to drop down the tower into a tank of water, forming small, perfectly round lead pellets. The building is now used as office space.

Turn right and after crossing the bridge turn left down the steps, now with the water on the left; shortly afterwards, cross a small bridge over the former moat of Bristol Castle to enter Castle Park. Built by the Normans, the castle was destroyed by Oliver Cromwell during the English Civil War in 1647; also in Castle Park are the ruins of St Peter's Church, which was bombed during World War II and is now preserved as a memorial.

Pero's Bridge at the Floating Harbour in Bristol is named after an 18th-century African slave

FLOATING HARBOUR

The Floating Harbour was created in 1809 by impounding (closing off with lock gates) a large area of the tidal River Avon so that ships remained afloat at all times. When it opened, it was the largest artificially impounded area of water in the world.

Following the closure of the commercial harbour in 1975, the area has been transformed, with art galleries, museums, cafés and bars occupying the former warehouses. Across Pero's Bridge and to the right is the tourist information centre and the Watershed film and digital media centre, while straight on leads to At-Bristol, an interactive hands-on science museum and 3D planetarium.

Across the A4 is Bristol Cathedral. Originally founded in 1140, the cathedral was partly rebuilt in the 14th century, with later Victorian alterations including the twin western towers.

On the south side of the Floating Harbour is the M Shed history museum, several preserved harbour cranes and the SS Great Britain. Designed by Isambard Kingdom Brunel, the SS Great Britain became, in 1845, the first propeller-driven iron-hulled steamship to cross the Atlantic.

Some 200 metres along Welsh Back, on the right, is King Street and the historic Llandoger Trow pub, which dates from 1664 (a 'trow' was a flat-bottomed boat).

Keep close to the water to reach a road beside Bristol Bridge (left), cross straight over the road and keep ahead for 30 metres before turning left along **Welsh Back** for 450 metres to a mini-roundabout. ◄ Turn right (left leads to Bristol Temple Meads railway station) and keep ahead through the tree-lined, early 18th-century **Queen Square**, with its equestrian statue of William III.

Cross over Prince Street and follow Farr's Lane to the **Floating Harbour**. Ahead is Pero's Bridge, named after an 18th-century African slave; its distinctive horn-shaped sculptures act as counterweights for the lifting section of the bridge. To the left is the youth hostel, the Arnolfini art gallery and a statue of John Cabot, who set sail from here in 1495 and discovered Newfoundland.

Turn right along the tree-shaded **Narrow Quay** to its end and continue straight on past the fountains to reach the statue of Neptune, the Roman god of the sea, marking the end of our meandering journey along the Kennet and Avon Canal.

Statue of Neptune at Bristol's Floating Harbour marks the end of the Kennet and Avon Canal walk

For Temple Meads railway station
Catch a ferry (from the landing stage just south of the fountains) or head back through Queen Square then east across Redcliffe Bridge. Keep left of the **Church of St Mary Redcliffe** (an 800-year-old Gothic masterpiece), following

the waymarked route along **Portwall Lane** to Temple Meads railway station (1.4km from statue of Neptune).

BRISTOL

The city of Bristol, which grew around the confluence of the Rivers Avon and Frome, has a long history stretching back to Neolithic times, confirmed by the discovery of flint tools. During the Iron Age, hill forts were built on surrounding high ground, and later there was a Roman settlement known as Portus Abonae at Sea Mills. By the Middle Ages, Bristol was known as Brycgstow, meaning 'place of the bridge'.

Bristol's growth and prosperity has been firmly linked with its docks since before the arrival of the Normans in the 11th century. Over the centuries, the port has traded in a range of goods, from cloth to sugar and wine, and played a part in the African slave trade during the 18th century. Nowadays, the main docks – Avonmouth and Royal Portbury – are further downstream facing the Bristol Channel, which has allowed the regeneration of the Floating Harbour into a vibrant cultural hub.

The city, England's sixth largest, is home to a wide range of tourist attractions and a full range of services. Aardman Animations who brought Morph, Wallace and Gromit and Shaun the Sheep to life are based in the city and the world-famous artist, Banksy, was born here. For a panoramic view across the city, take a walk up to Cabot Tower, crowning Brandon Hill Park. Visit the Georgian House (0117 921 1362) for a look at an Edwardian sugar plantation owner's house from the 1790s, or opt for the city museum and art gallery (0117 922 3571).

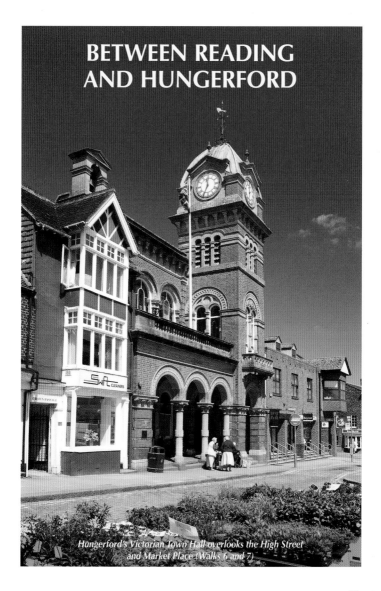

BETWEEN READING
AND HUNGERFORD

*Hungerford's Victorian Town Hall overlooks the High Street
and Market Place (Walks 6 and 7)*

WALK 1

Reading – canal and river

Start/finish	Reading railway station, north (Caversham) exit (SU 714 738); parking available nearby
Distance	6.8km (4¼ miles)
Total ascent	45m
Time	2hr
Map	OS Explorer 159
Refreshments	Numerous choices in Reading
Public transport	Trains to Reading; extensive bus links
Note	The walk may also be started from Hills Meadow pay-and-display car park (SU 718 741), on the B3345 just north of Reading Bridge.

An easy half-day walk, following parts of the Thames Path and canal towpath and taking in the junction of the Kennet and Avon Canal and the River Thames, before meandering through parts of Reading.

The town is often known for the 'Three Bs' of Beer, Bulbs and Biscuits: Simonds' Brewery was established by William Blackall Simonds in 1785 (it was taken over by Courage and closed soon after in 2010); Suttons Seeds was founded in 1806 by John Sutton to provide corn seed and expanded into flower and vegetable seeds in 1837 (the company moved to Devon in 1976); and Huntley & Palmers biscuits. Joseph Huntley opened a small biscuit bakery here in 1822, and in 1841 George Palmer became a partner, to form Huntley & Palmers – by 1900 the company was the largest biscuit manufacturer in the world (biscuit production in Reading came to an end in 1976).

From the north (Caversham) exit of Reading railway station, follow the waymarked walking/cycle route northwards past the bus stops along Trooper Potts Way. Cross over the **A329** at the traffic lights, turn right for a few metres and then turn left along Norman Place (signposted to Christchurch Meadows and Caversham) to reach the **River Thames**. ▶

Turn left along the Thames Path (with the river on your right) for 650 metres, ignoring the combined cycle/pedestrian bridge. This bridge can be used as a shortcut, reducing the walk by 1.4km. On the right is **Fry's Island**, also known as De Montfort Island following a trial by combat between Robert de Montfort and Henry of Essex in 1163. Just before **Caversham Bridge** (A4155), fork left to the road (the Thames Path goes straight on) and turn right to cross the river. The first bridge across the Thames here, built in the 12th century, housed a small chapel dedicated to St Anne; the current bridge dates from the 1920s.

Once across the bridge, turn right along Promenade Road to its end. Keep ahead along the tarmac path, following the river downstream through Christchurch Meadows and soon passing under the combined cycle/ pedestrian bridge again. Keep ahead under Reading Bridge (**B3345**), passing Whittington's Tea Barge, and continue alongside the river with **Hills Meadow car park** on the left. This is an alternative start/finish point.

Keep the river on the right, fork right at the split and turn right at the path junction. Cross a footbridge onto Heron Island, bear right to cross another footbridge onto **View Island** and keep ahead. ▶

Follow the path over the weir, then cross **Caversham Lock**. Turn left and follow the Thames Path for 1.2km, passing through **King's Meadow** and staying close to the river. At **Kennet Mouth**, where the Kennet and Avon Canal and River Kennet join the River Thames, follow the Thames Path across the River Kennet and canal via the wooden Horseshoe Bridge. Turn sharp left and double back under the bridge, following the canal, and pass under two railway bridges. ▶

Keep to the canalside path for 800 metres, soon with flats on the left, passing the Jolly Anglers pub, **Blake's**

The Thames, which rises in Gloucestershire, is England's longest river, meandering for 346km (215 miles) through eight counties before reaching the North Sea.

A path to the left takes a short loop round View Island.

Isambard Kingdom Brunel's Great Western Railway, between London and Bristol, arrived here in 1840.

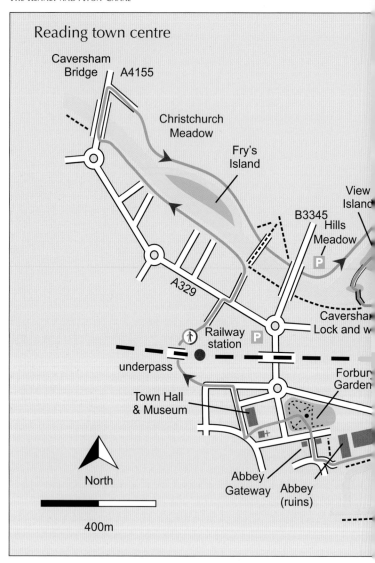

Reading town centre

Caversham Bridge — A4155

Christchurch Meadow

Fry's Island

View Island

B3345

Hills Meadow

P

A329

Railway station

P

underpass

Caversham Lock and w

Forbury Garden

Town Hall & Museum

North

400m

Abbey Gateway

Abbey (ruins)

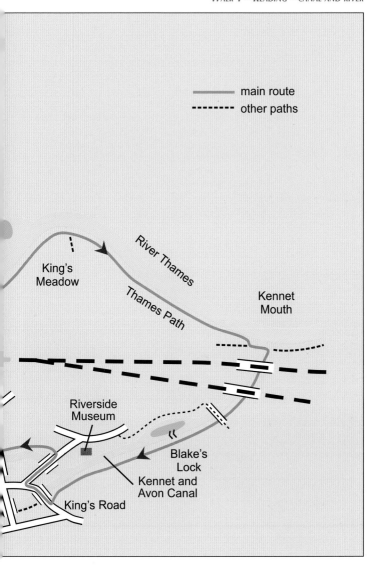

main route

------- other paths

King's Meadow

River Thames

Thames Path

Kennet Mouth

Riverside Museum

Blake's Lock

Kennet and Avon Canal

King's Road

Lock (this is the first, or last, lock along the Kennet and Avon Canal) and then the Fisherman's Cottage pub. Just before the road bridge, go up the steps and turn right along **King's Road**, crossing the canal. After passing the last remaining part of the former Huntley & Palmers biscuit factory, turn right along Gas Works Road. Cross the bridge and immediately turn left; ahead, on the right, past the Bel & the Dragon pub, is the **Riverside Museum** (accessed through the car park). ◄

This small museum gives a brief insight into Reading's two rivers: the Kennet and the Thames.

Follow the path, with the River Kennet on the left. Pass under the low bridge (A329) and dogleg right up the slight ramp to continue along the tree-lined Chestnut Walk (with memorial gates and seat dedicated to Oscar Wilde) between the river (left) and former Victorian Reading Prison (right).

Looking upstream along the River Thames at Christchurch Meadows

The playwright, poet and novelist **Oscar Wilde** was imprisoned here in the late 1800s. Following his

release in 1897, he wrote The Ballad of Reading Gaol, a poem inspired by his prison experience.

Continue past the southern end of the ruins of **Reading Abbey** (right) and follow the tarmac drive to the right as it skirts round the office block, turning right at the junction beside the tall office building (The Blade) to pass through the **Abbey Gateway**; in the late 18th century, this housed a school where the romantic novelist Jane Austen and her sister Cassandra studied.

The once great Norman **abbey**, founded by Henry I in 1121, came to dominate the town for over four centuries until Henry VIII's Dissolution of the Monasteries; Henry I is said to be buried within the abbey ruins. The building was of a similar size to Westminster Abbey (London) and in medieval times was one of the wealthiest abbeys in the country. Today, some flint rubble walls, the hospitium and the Abbey Gateway are all that remain. The abbey is recorded as the site where Britain's earliest four-part harmony with verse was written – 'Sumer is icumen in' (c.1250).

Cross over the road (to the left is the Trooper Potts Memorial, in memory of Frederick Owen Potts, Reading's only Victoria Cross holder) to enter the **Forbury Gardens** (café on right). Follow the second path on the left to reach the large monument, the Maiwand Lion.

The **Maiwand Lion** monument, erected in 1886 and designed by George Blackall Simonds (member of the famous brewing family and an accomplished sculptor), commemorates the men of the 66th Berkshire Regiment who fell during the Battles of Maiwand and Kandahar at the end of the second Afghan War (1878–80). The Forbury Gardens, laid out by the Victorians, originally formed the outer court of the abbey; the cross to the south-east commemorates Henry I.

The imposing Maiwand Lion in the Forbury Gardens

The statue, erected in 1902, is of King Edward VIII.

Continue a few metres past the monument to a cross-path junction and turn left. Leave the gardens, cross over The Forbury (road) and follow the path through the churchyard; over to the right is the hospitium, or dormitory, of the former abbey. Continue alongside St Laurence's Church to reach Town Hall Square, overlooked by the red-and-grey-brick Victorian Gothic-style **Town Hall and Museum**.

Reading Museum (0118 937 3400) gives an insight into the history of the town and has artefacts from the nearby Roman town of Calleva Atrebatum and a late 19th-century copy of the Bayeux Tapestry. A statue of Queen Victoria by George Blackall Simonds stands in Town Hall Square, erected in 1887 to celebrate her Golden Jubilee. Inside St Laurence's Church, parts of which date back to Norman times, there is a monument to the Reading mathematician John Blagrave, who designed the 'Mathematical Jewel' – a complex type of armillary sphere sundial – in 1585.

Turn right (northwards) along Blagrave Street (museum on right), ignore Valpy Street on the right and at the next junction cross over Forbury Road. Turn left and soon bear right to the main entrance of the **railway station**. ◀ For the northern exit (where the walk began), follow the signed route for the River Thames and Caversham down the steps. Turn right through the underpass and bear right.

WALK 2

Aldermaston – wharf and village

Start/finish	Aldermaston railway station (SU 601 673); pay and display parking is available at the station and beside the canal visitor centre along Wharfside in Aldermaston Wharf (SU 602 972), 500 metres south of A4 along A340
Distance	9.1km (5¾ miles)
Total ascent	65m
Time	2½hr
Map	OS Explorer 159
Refreshments	Aldermaston Wharf: tea room at the canal visitor centre (0118 971 2868), the Butt Inn (0118 971 3309 – short detour); Aldermaston: the Hind's Head (0118 971 2194), shop
Public transport	Trains to Aldermaston Wharf (Aldermaston station); daily bus services to A4 near Aldermaston Wharf from Reading and Newbury
Note	To start from the visitor centre and tea room head south to the canal, then turn right to the A340 and turn left.

From Aldermaston Wharf, which dates from the opening of the Kennet Navigation between Reading and Newbury in 1724, the walk heads southwards to cross the River Kennet and then follows Fisherman's Lane towards Aldermaston. After a quick circuit of the village, passing the church and pub, the route meanders alongside the River Kennet before following the canal back to the start.

Exit from Platform 2 (westbound), follow the entrance road through the parking area and turn left along Station Road. Cross over the A340 and turn right to the canal; 100 metres to the left is the visitor centre and tea room (housed in a former canal worker's cottage). After crossing the canal, turn left into Mill Lane and then take the

To allow salmon to migrate along the river once again, a number of salmon ladders (fish passes) have been built beside weirs.

right-hand track, heading south-east for 600 metres towards Padworth Mill.

Fork right just before the entrance to Mill House (footpath sign), following an enclosed path. Cross several footbridges over the River Kennet; look left for a view of the former mill shortly before passing the salmon ladder. ◄

Go through a gate and keep ahead between fences before crossing a footbridge and going through another gate to a **four-way path junction** in the field. Turn right along the track (Fisherman's Lane), keeping ahead through gates. After 1.1km pass a cottage (right) and keep ahead for 350 metres, following the hedge-lined track (not the private field track). At the footpath sign turn left over a stile (SU 595 655).

Follow the left-hand field edge, cross a stile in the corner and keep ahead, passing just left of a barn. Follow

Padworth Mill stands on the River Kennet near Aldermaston Wharf

the right-hand fence line uphill to a stile in the top right corner beside a gate. Cross over the road and turn right; a short distance to the left is the **Church of St Mary the Virgin**.

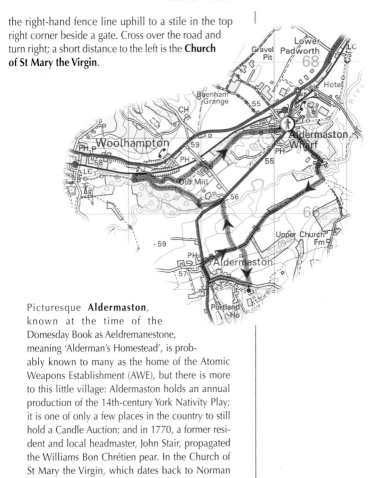

Picturesque **Aldermaston**, known at the time of the Domesday Book as Aeldremanestone, meaning 'Alderman's Homestead', is probably known to many as the home of the Atomic Weapons Establishment (AWE), but there is more to this little village: Aldermaston holds an annual production of the 14th-century York Nativity Play; it is one of only a few places in the country to still hold a Candle Auction; and in 1770, a former resident and local headmaster, John Stair, propagated the Williams Bon Chrétien pear. In the Church of St Mary the Virgin, which dates back to Norman times, there are several memorials to past lords of the manor, including the fine alabaster tomb of Sir George Forster and his wife (c.1530).

Aldermaston Manor was once the home of William Congreve, a relation of the Restoration dramatist of the same name. The wrought-iron gates

at the former entrance (North Lodge) – known as
the Eagle Gates – are said to have been won by him
in a card game in the early 19th century; the gates
originally belonged to Midgham Manor.

Follow the road down towards **Aldermaston**, passing
the entrance to Aldermaston Park. Keep right at the junction, beside the triangular-shaped village green – known
as The Loosey – overlooked by the red-brick North Lodge
and the Eagle Gates on the left. Head down The Street
(A340), lined with 17th- and 18th-century cottages,
towards the Hind's Head pub.

At the mini-roundabout, in front of the Hind's Head
(originally a 17th-century coaching inn), turn right along
the track, passing to the right of the shop, and follow the
track (Fisherman's Lane) for 500 metres (soon crossing
Maida's Way). At the footpath sign (SU 594 655), turn left
through a gate in the hedge.

Head northwards through three fields separated by
two footbridges with gates. At the far side of the third
field, go through a gate, cross a footbridge and keep
ahead through another gate. Bear right along the tarmac cycleway to the main road (A340) beside a bridge.
Turn left (verge) for 50 metres and then go right across
the road. Go down some steps and through a gate, and
bear diagonally left following a permissive path through
the field; on the right is the River Kennet, with the **Old
Mill** (built around 1800 and originally a flour mill) on the
opposite bank.

In the far right corner of the field, go right across
the bridge over the River Enborne and keep ahead to the
River Kennet (this area can flood in the winter). Bear left
along the riverbank. Where the river joins the canal, bear
diagonally left through trees (marker post) before shortly
rejoining the canal and following the canalside path.
Cross over the canal at the footbridge (30) and head east,
with the canal on the right; over to the left is the railway.

Follow the towpath for 2.5km back to Aldermaston
Wharf, crossing from the left-hand to the right-hand
side of the canal at Frouds Bridge (29). Keep ahead past

Aldermaston Lock (95) with its unusual scalloped brick-work, to reach the A340 at **Aldermaston Wharf**; the Butt Inn is 200 metres to the right.

Heading east along the canal back towards Aldermaston

When the River Kennet between Reading and Newbury was made navigable in the 1720s, **Aldermaston Wharf** was built and the area developed into a busy trading centre. Aldermaston Lock used to be known as Brewhouse Lock because the Aldermaston Brewery – later called Strange's Brewery – once stood to the south of the lock. The brewery buildings were demolished in the 1950s.

Turn left across the canal and fork left along Station Road, retracing the route back to the station.

WALK 3
Greenham Common

Start/finish	Thatcham railway station (SU 527 663); pay-and-display parking
Distance	12.7km (8 miles); shorter route: minus 3.1km (2 miles)
Total ascent	100m; shorter route: minus 5m
Time	3½hr; shorter route: minus 1hr
Map	OS Explorer 158
Refreshments	Thatcham: the Swan (01635 862084); Nature Discovery Centre: café (01635 874381, off route)
Public transport	Trains to Thatcham; bus services to Thatcham railway station from Newbury and Tilehurst (excluding Sundays)
Note	The walk may also be started from the car park at Greenham Common (SU 498 651) on Bury Banks Road, 2.7km east along Pinchington Lane off the A339.

An interesting walk to the south of Thatcham, in an area that has a rich and varied wildlife and a history stretching back to the Stone Age. The walk sets out from the railway station, following the canal westwards towards Newbury and passing the turf-sided Monkey Marsh Lock. On the way, a short detour gives access to the Nature Discovery Centre with its important reedbed habitats.

Soon the canal is left behind as the walk heads south, passing the ancient woodland of Bowdown Woods Nature Reserve, to arrive at Greenham Common. Once associated with the Cold War and protests about nuclear weapons, a large part of this former airbase has been returned to open heath and is home to a wide variety of wildlife. After taking in a sweeping loop around the common (the shorter walk takes in less of the common), the route heads north to cross the River Kennet before heading east along the canal back to the start.

Exit the railway station from Platform 1 and head to the main road (a short way to the right is the Swan pub). Cross over the road and follow the towpath westwards (with the canal to your left) to reach Monkey Marsh Lock (90) after 300 metres; this is one of only two remaining turf-sided locks along the canal, the other being Garston Lock (102). Keep alongside the canal for 1.6km to Widmead Lock (89); from here a short detour leads to the **Nature Discovery Centre** (800 metres each way).

Detour to the Nature Discovery Centre
Just after passing Widmead Lock, turn right through a gate and follow the enclosed path. Take great care as you cross the railway, and keep ahead to a track junction (the track to the left leads to Thatcham Reedbeds). Continue northwards along the lakeside path (with the lake on your right) to reach the centre and café (nature trails and car park); retrace your steps and turn right along the canal.

The **Nature Discovery Centre**, managed by Berks, Bucks & Oxon Wildlife Trust (BBOWT), consists of several flooded gravel pits that provide a habitat for a wide variety of wildlife, from damselflies and dragonflies to common terns. The adjacent **Thatcham Reedbeds** reserve, one of the largest

Take a short detour to visit the wetland habitats and café at the Nature Discovery Centre

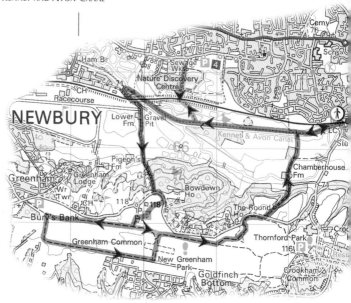

areas of inland reedbed in southern England, is home to warblers (reed, sedge and Cetti's) and the diminutive Desmoulin's snail.

Continue westwards along the canal, soon passing under the **railway bridge**, then keep left over a footbridge to reach Bull's Lock (88). Just after the lock, cross the canal via the swing bridge (48), keep ahead to a lane and turn left, soon passing under the **railway** again. Here the road splits; take the right-hand lane, which soon swings right (on the right you catch a glimpse of **Newbury Racecourse**, which opened in 1905) to pass **Lower Farm**.

Continue along the track, which later heads uphill and passes Bowdown Farmhouse; on the left is BBOWT's **Bowdown Woods Nature Reserve**, with areas of ancient woodland and a varied wildlife (waymarked trails meander through the reserve).

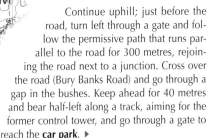

Continue uphill; just before the road, turn left through a gate and follow the permissive path that runs parallel to the road for 300 metres, rejoining the road next to a junction. Cross over the road (Bury Banks Road) and go through a gap in the bushes. Keep ahead for 40 metres and bear half-left along a track, aiming for the former control tower, and go through a gate to reach the **car park**. ▶

This is an alternative start/finish point for the walk.

Turn left (south) past the control tower (now a visitor centre and cafe), go through a gate to a track junction and turn right. For the shorter walk, turn left for 300 metres to a junction (SU 501 648) and rejoin the main walk heading east.

Follow the gravel track westwards to a junction and keep left, then follow the track as it swings left with the former silos on the right. Keep to the track for 1.5km to a junction and turn left, crossing where the centre of the runway was, to reach another junction (SU 501 648) not far from the control tower and turn right. ▶

This is where the shorter walk rejoins the main walk.

The airfield at **Greenham Common** was built during World War II, but it was during the Cold War that Greenham became a household name. Rising tensions between NATO and the Soviet Union led to ground-launched nuclear cruise missiles being deployed here, which in turn gave rise to the Greenham Common Women's Peace Camp during the 1980s; on two occasions, between 30,000 and 50,000 women circled the perimeter fence.

Following the nuclear non-proliferation treaty, the airfield was declared redundant in 1992, and in 2000, after decades of military use, the common was officially reopened for public use. Most of the military structures have been removed, except for the central part of the single east–west runway that originally stretched for 3.6km, the reinforced-concrete silos that housed the cruise missiles, and the old control tower.

Sunset over Greenham Common, once home to nuclear cruise missiles

Managed by BBOWT, the common offers a varied wildlife, including over 30 species of butterfly, rare birds such as the nightjar and Dartford warbler, and a range of plants, including several species of orchid.

Follow the track eastwards for 1.2km to a junction and fork left for 900 metres. Head through the trees and follow the track as it curves clockwise, soon with a road over to the left and pits on the right, to reach a marker post. Turn left and leave the common through a gate (SU 516 650).

Worked flints dating from the Stone Age have been found close to the river around here.

Cross over the road and follow the track (bridleway) opposite, going downhill for 500 metres. Bear left along the tarmac track and cross the River Kennet. ◄ Keep ahead past the buildings at **Chamberhouse Farm** and follow the track for 500 metres to reach the canal. Cross over via the swing bridge and turn right alongside the canal for 600 metres, retracing the route back to the railway station.

WALK 4

Newbury and Donnington

Start/finish	Newbury Wharf (SU 473 672); pay-and-display parking accessed along Wharf Road just off the A339 in Newbury, near the library
Alternative start/finish	Newbury railway station (SU 472 667)
Distance	7.6km (4¾ miles); alternative start/finish: add 0.8km (½ mile)
Total ascent	90m; alternative start/finish: add 0m
Time	2hr; alternative start/finish: add ¼hr
Map	OS Explorer 158
Refreshments	Lots of choice in Newbury
Public transport	Trains to Newbury; good local bus connections
Note	The walk may also be started from the car park on the B4494 opposite the Castle pub (SU 466 687) or from Donnington Castle (SU 461 690).

From Newbury's old wharf, with its canalside tea shop and restored wharfside crane, the walk heads north across the canal and through Victoria Park, before crossing the River Lambourn to arrive at historic Shaw House. Then it's off for a quick look at the stark ruins of Donnington Castle before heading south to recross the River Lambourn on the way to Speen. Here, the walk joins the Lambourn Valley Way for a while, passing a 'holy well', before heading east along the canal, back to bustling Newbury with its 'wool church' and museum.

Alternative start from the railway station
Exit from Platform 2 (north exit) and turn right along Cheap Street as it soon swings left. Keep ahead at junctions to enter the Market Place and head to the far right corner. Turn right along Wharf Street past the museum and turn left to the wharf.

Lions guard the statue of Queen Victoria in Newbury's Victoria Park

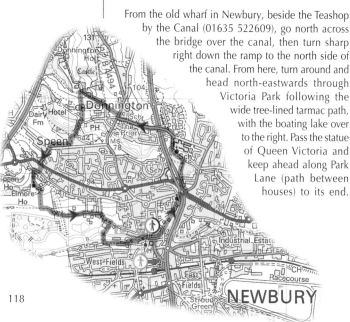

From the old wharf in Newbury, beside the Teashop by the Canal (01635 522609), go north across the bridge over the canal, then turn sharp right down the ramp to the north side of the canal. From here, turn around and head north-eastwards through Victoria Park following the wide tree-lined tarmac path, with the boating lake over to the right. Pass the statue of Queen Victoria and keep ahead along Park Lane (path between houses) to its end.

Go through the underpass and bear left, cross the B4009 (Shaw Road) at the lights and turn left (signposted to Donnington) along the pavement as it curves right, to follow the A339 for 175 metres. Dogleg right and continue along the enclosed path in the same direction. Cross a footbridge and head through the small park, keeping to the right-hand side. Cross over the River Lambourn and follow the path to reach a road (Church Road), with Shaw House opposite.

> The Elizabethan **Shaw House**, an important example of an early symmetrical H-plan mansion, was built in 1581 by Thomas Dolman, whose family had made their fortune in the cloth trade. The house had a number of owners before becoming a school until 1985. Now owned by West Berkshire Council, the house and café are open to the public at various times (01635 279279).

Turn left along the road, passing St Mary's Church (built in 1840), then Trinity School to reach a junction (mini-roundabout). Cross over the road (Love Lane) and

The path arrives at Church Road, with a view of Elizabethan Shaw House opposite

turn left along the pavement for 800 metres, crossing the bridge over the A339, to arrive at a crossroads with Oxford Road (B4494) in **Donnington**, beside the Castle pub (01635 40615).

Turn right past the pub and then left across the B4494 to enter the cricket and recreation ground, just to the right of a small car park (alternative start). Follow the signposted path westwards before heading for a gate in the top (north-west) corner, to the right of the clubhouse. Turn left and then right along the tarmac drive to a parking area (alternative start) below **Donnington Castle** and turn left; the gate gives access to the castle.

The gatehouse is all that remains of the 14th-century Donnington Castle

Donnington Castle was constructed by Sir Richard Abberbury in the late 14th century and originally consisted of a curtain wall with four round corner-towers and a substantial gatehouse. During the English Civil War, the Royalist castle was attacked on a number of occasions before surrendering to

The walk heads through the landscaped parkland of Donnington Grove

the Parliamentarians. Today, only the stark twin-towered gatehouse remains. From this vantage point there are views south across the Kennet Valley to the North Hampshire Downs.

Follow the path along the top edge of the car park (with the castle on your right) to a path junction (marker post) beside some trees. Turn left downhill, following the trees on the left. Bear left along the tarmac drive and keep ahead (south) at the junction to cross a bridge, with views to the right across the lake at Donnington Grove.

Cross the bridge over the River Lambourn, keep ahead to a crossing track and bear right then left along a waymarked path, heading south across the golf course to a path junction, with a gate and road beyond. Stay within the golf course and turn right for 300 metres before turning left and leaving through a gate. Turn right along Grove Road for a few metres and then left across the road and follow Station Road in **Speen** up to a T-junction; opposite is the Hare and Hounds pub (01635 521152).

121

Cross over and turn left for 50 metres, then turn right along the path between brick walls. At the end of the path, turn right along the lane for 75 metres and then turn left down the byway, following the Lambourn Valley Way (LVW). After 50 metres, detour right to visit the Lady Well. ◄

This 'holy well' is said to date from Roman times or possibly earlier.

Continue downhill, go through the lychgate, then follow the path through the churchyard, keeping to the left of St Mary's Church.

Speen, mentioned in a Saxon charter in AD821, has been suggested by some as the location of the Roman settlement of Spinis (Spinae); however, Bronze Age artefacts found locally suggest that its history goes back much further. During the English Civil War, the Second Battle of Newbury was fought here on 27 October 1644 (the First Battle of Newbury was fought to the south-west at Wash Common, in 1643). St Mary's Church has Saxon origins, although it was mostly rebuilt by the Victorians; Queen Elizabeth I's Italian tutor Giovanni Battista Castiglione (who was granted Benham Valence manor in 1570) is buried here.

Turn left up the drive for 75 metres to a signpost and turn right through the gate. Follow the path (LVW) south between open fields to a path junction. Turn left, soon going through a gate, and then follow the track ahead under the disused railway bridge, built to carry the Lambourn Valley Railway, which opened in 1898. Keep ahead along the track for 500 metres to its end at Goldwell Park and turn right along the tarmac path, which soon swings left.

Pass a car park and follow Northcroft Lane. Just after passing the leisure centre, turn right and follow the tarmac path. Cross a footbridge, then another footbridge (63) over the canal and head east along the towpath towards **Newbury** (canal on the left). Continue along the lane with cottages on the right, ignore Kennet Road (right) and follow West Mills for a few metres before going left over the swing bridge (62). Immediately turn right along the towpath (canal on right), soon passing Newbury Lock (85); on the left is a sculpture called Ebb and Flow, by Peter Randall-Page, which fills and empties with the movement of water through the lock. Follow the way-marked path past the Lock, Stock and Barrel pub (01635 580550) to join Bridge Street.

> The busy town of **Newbury** has, throughout its history, had important transport links, ranging from its earliest days as a safe crossing point over the River Kennet to when stagecoaches travelled between London and Bath along the Great Bath Road (now the A4), followed by the opening of the canal and then the arrival of the railway in 1847.
>
> In the late 15th century, the cloth trade had brought wealth to the town and Newbury's most famous clothier was John Smallwood (or Winchcombe), better known as 'Jack of Newbury'. St Nicolas' Church is a great example of an early 16th-century 'wool church', built in the Perpendicular style, with high windows and a pinnacled tower (wool churches were built primarily from the proceeds of the medieval wool trade). Inside the church there are several interesting features, including an early 17th-century Jacobean pulpit and a memorial to Newbury's famous clothier, John Smallwood.
>
> To learn more about Newbury and the area, head for the West Berkshire Museum (01635 519562) housed in the former 17th-century Granary and Cloth Hall.

Turn right over the bridge to a junction; 25 metres ahead on the right is St Nicolas' Church. Turn left, keep left through the Market Place and follow Wharf Street, passing the West Berkshire Museum (right) to a junction; turn left back to the start.

WALK 5

Kintbury and Hamstead Marshall

Start/finish	Kintbury railway station (SU 386 671); car park on the opposite side of the road beside the canal, 1.2km south of the A4 between Newbury and Hungerford
Distance	9.6km (6 miles)
Total ascent	125m
Time	2¾hr
Map	OS Explorer 158
Refreshments	Kintbury: the Dundas Arms (01488 658263), plus off route in the village the Blue Ball (01488 608126), Cocochoux Cake Café (01488 658717) and shop
Public transport	Trains to Kintbury; bus services to Kintbury from Newbury and Hungerford (excluding Sundays)

From Kintbury railway station and the picturesque canalside Dundas Arms pub, the walk follows a short section of the canal to Shepherd's Bridge before heading south-eastwards over Irish Hill to reach Hamstead Marshall. The walk soon passes several pairs of gateposts, all that remain of a once grand mansion, before rejoining the canal which is followed back to the start.

> To explore the village of **Kintbury**, head south from the canal for 175 metres along Station Road, then turn right along the waymarked path to Church Street, with the picturesque St Mary's Church opposite. The church dates from the 12th century and houses several interesting monuments. Turn left along Church Street to a crossroads beside the village shop and Cocochoux Cake Café (located in Thatcher's Yard) – 150 metres to the right is the Blue Ball pub – then turn left down Station Road back to the canal.

From Kintbury railway station, turn left along the road. Just before the canal bridge, turn left to join the towpath;

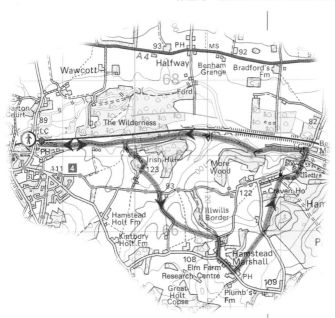

across the canal is the 18th-century canalside Dundas Arms pub. Head east along the canal for 1.2km to Shepherd's Bridge (73) and turn right across the canal. Here the path splits; take the left fork over the stile and head up **Irish Hill**, keeping close to the right-hand field edge. Cross the stile at the top and continue along the track to a signed junction. Keep ahead, heading southeast (the main track forks right) to enter a field, and continue in the same direction down across the field passing a solitary tree on the way. At the lower field edge, go through the trees to a minor road and junction.

Cross over and follow the lane straight on (southeast) for 450 metres; where the lane swings right, go left over a stile. Follow the waymarked path across the fields, ignoring a crossing path (track) and then another crossing track to reach a stile and path junction at the corner of a

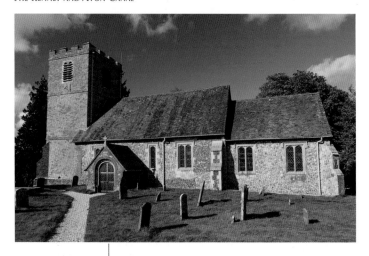

St Mary's Church,
Hamstead Marshall

wood. Cross over the stile and keep ahead through the next field, aiming just left of the distant house, to reach a stile. Turn right along the lane to a three-way junction. Turn left following the road through **Hamstead Marshall** for 300 metres – there is no pavement so take care as the road is narrow – to reach a track on the left, opposite the **Elm Farm Organic Research Centre**.

The original part of **Hamstead Marshall** lies to the north, close to the banks of the River Kennet. The village dates back to at least Saxon times, although the first written evidence appears in the Domesday Book of 1086, when it was held by a Norman, Hugolin the Steersman. Hamstead's importance started to grow in the early 12th century when it became the seat of John FitzGilbert the Marshal, one of the monarch's chief advisers, who was given the title of Earl Marshal; this title later passed to his son, William.

The manor passed through a succession of owners and in the early 17th century was acquired by the Craven family. In 1661, the 1st Earl of Craven commissioned the Dutch architect Sir Balthazar Gerbier to design and build a grand mansion. Unfortunately the house was short-lived as it was extensively damaged by a great fire in 1718 and was later demolished; all that remain today are several pairs of elaborate gateposts. St Mary's Church, parts of which date from the 12th century with later additions, houses a memorial to Gerbier.

A quick look at the map reveals that there are three mottes, or earth mounds, near the church that were built as motte-and-bailey castles during the late 11th or early 12th century.

Turn left along the track (bridleway). Pass some farm buildings and keep ahead for 650 metres between the fields before going through a gate next to a seat. Cross over Park Lane and follow the signed path up the bank and through a gate. Go up across the field heading northwards and through another gate. Continue straight

Several sets of gateposts are all that remain of a once grand mansion, Hamstead Marshall

Looking east along the canal near Irish Hill

To visit St Mary's Church, go through the gate in the brick wall; after visiting the church, retrace your steps back to the footpath sign and turn left.

on with a fence on the right for 350 metres; beyond the fence is an earth ditch and bank referred to as a 'Park Pale' – the remains of a medieval deer-park boundary.

On drawing level with some trees on the right, bear half-left and head northwards across the field aiming for the **church**, passing just left of a pair of gateposts (once belonging to Hamstead's grand mansion); over to the right are another set of gateposts. Go through a gate to reach a signed path junction beside another pair of gateposts in front of the churchyard wall and turn right (east). ◀

Follow the track, which soon curves down to the left. Turn left along the driveway and leave through a gate beside the cattle grid. Turn right along the road past Hamstead Mill, crossing the bridge over the River Kennet. Immediately after crossing the canal, turn left to join the towpath beside the lock (81).

The walk now follows the canal for 3.8km westwards back to **Kintbury**, passing two locks and Shepherd's Bridge (73).

Just before the bridge, below Irish Hill, was the site of an early 20th-century **whiting mill**, where chalk was ground into a fine powder for use in various products, including paint.

WALK 6
Hungerford and Kintbury

Start/finish	Hungerford railway station (SU 340 685); parking (pay and display) in Station Road (SU 339 685) near the railway station
Distance	11.6km (7¼ miles)
Total ascent	105m
Time	3¼hr
Map	OS Explorer 158
Refreshments	Hungerford: lots of choice; Kintbury: the Dundas Arms (01488 658263), the Blue Ball (01488 608126), Cocochoux Cake Café (01488 658717), shop
Public transport	Railway stations at Hungerford and Kintbury; bus services between Hungerford, Kintbury and Newbury (except Sundays)

After leaving Hungerford's railway station, the walk follows the canal eastwards, running parallel with the railway and meeting up with the River Kennet on several occasions to arrive at the picturesque village of Kintbury. After a quick meander through the village, home to a couple of pubs and a 12th-century church, the route heads past St Cassian's on its way through fields back towards Hungerford, with distant views of the North Hampshire Downs. The final section heads across Hungerford Common back to the railway station. If you have time, the market town of Hungerford is well worth exploring.

Exit the railway station from Platform 1, turn right down the lane to the canal and turn right along the towpath. The walk now follows the towpath eastwards for 5km to Kintbury, following the south side to Dunmill Lock (75) and then crossing over via the road bridge to follow the north bank. ▶

The River Kennet meets up with the canal for the first time here on its journey to Reading.

Just before **Dunmill Lock**, the 18th-century Dun Mill can be seen on the opposite bank (there was

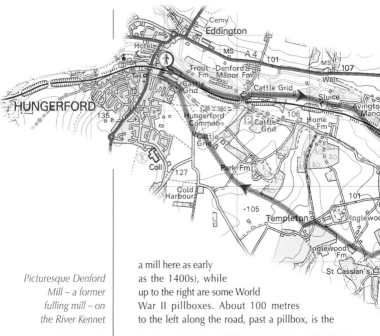

Picturesque Denford Mill – a former fulling mill – on the River Kennet

a mill here as early as the 1400s), while up to the right are some World War II pillboxes. About 100 metres to the left along the road, past a pillbox, is the

picturesque Denford Mill (private house) straddling
the River Kennet; this was once a fulling mill, where
rough woven cloth was cleaned and thickened.

Continue alongside the
canal, passing three locks (76,
77 and 78), to reach a road
bridge at **Kintbury** (just
to the left is a car park
and railway station).
Turn right across
the canal, with the
Dundas Arms on
the left. Follow the
road past the former
Kintbury Mill (pri-
vate) and the junction
with Mill Bank (both on
the right), continue for
75 metres, then head up
the ramp and turn right along
the signed footpath. Follow the
tarmac path (The Cliffs) past the
houses and gardens, keeping ahead at
the footpath junction to pass an old turn-
stile. Cross slightly left over Church Lane and go through
the gate to enter the churchyard. Keep ahead to a cross-
junction, with St Mary's Church to the right, and turn left
to leave the churchyard.

Kintbury was first mentioned in Saxon times, when
it was known as Cynetanbrig. St Mary's Church
dates from the 12th century and houses several
interesting monuments, including one by the
Flemish sculptor Scheemakers and an early 17th-
century brass. A local legend mentions the Kintbury
Great Bell, which supposedly sank into the River
Kennet; many attempts were made to retrieve it, but
all failed and the bell has remained hidden in the

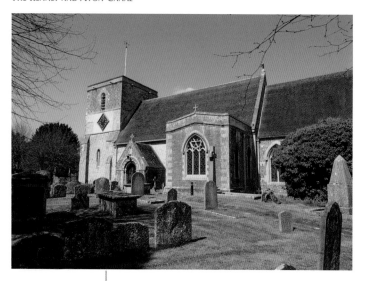

The walk passes through the churchyard of 12th-century St Mary's Church, Kintbury

This was known as the Manor of Wallingtons after Robert de Wallington acquired the manor in the 13th century; the present building dates from the early 17th century.

river ever since. The novelist Jane Austen visited the village on a number of occasions.

Keep ahead along Church Street to the crossroads (Cocochoux Cake Café – located in Thatcher's Yard – and village shop on the right) and turn right along the High Street for 200 metres. Some 20 metres after passing the Blue Ball pub, fork left along Wallingtons Road for 600 metres. On reaching a gated entrance (signposted private driveway to St Cassian's) beside a house, fork left along the track for 200 metres to a farm building on the left. Turn right here through a gate and continue west-south-west across the field. Pass through gates either side of a driveway and continue through the next field in the same direction, passing just left of some trees. Keep ahead through a belt of trees, then go through a gate and continue to a signed four-way path junction mid-field, with **St Cassian's** beyond. ◄

Turn right, keep left of trees surrounding an old quarry, cross the concrete track and keep ahead. Go through a gate and continue through the next field, before passing gates either side of a surfaced drive, with **Inglewood Farm** to the left. Continue through the field, passing some trees, then go through a gate in the field corner next to a wooden pylon.

Follow the right-hand field boundary, go through a gate and follow the enclosed path to a lane at **Templeton**. Turn left along the lane for 150 metres, then turn right through a wide gap in the hedge and follow the grassy strip across the field. Cross a footbridge and continue along the enclosed path, with a plantation on the right. Pass a gate and keep straight on through two fields (separated by a track), following the right-hand field boundary to a gate. ▶

Go through the gate to enter **Hungerford Common** (open access land) and follow the left-hand boundary to a road beside a cattle grid.

Hungerford Common – officially Common Port Down – is an area of open grassland on the eastern

Views to the south take in the North Hampshire Downs and the double gibbet on Inkpen Hill.

View of 17th-century St Cassian's, near Kintbury

edge of Hungerford, grazed by commoner's cattle. The name 'Port Down' is derived from the Saxon and French word *porte* (gate) and the Saxon word *dun* (hill), giving 'gated hill' or 'gated down', and there are still gates (and now cattle grids) at all entrances to the common.

The common is managed by the Town and Manor of Hungerford, who also oversee the annual Hocktide Festival, the main event of which is Tutti Day (second Tuesday after Easter), marking the end of the financial and administrative year. On Tutti Day, commoners attend the Hocktide Court and two Tutti Men visit every house with common rights.

Cross over the road. Here the path splits: take the right-hand fork heading north-north-west across the open common to reach a road on the edge of **Hungerford** beside a car park and the Down Gate pub. Keep ahead along Park Street for 250 metres and turn right down Station Road back to the railway station.

To visit **Hungerford**, keep ahead along Park Street to reach the High Street (A388) near the Town Hall. Places of interest include St Lawrence's Church, dating from 1816 and built from Bath stone brought here via the canal; and the Bear Hotel (at the junction of the A388 and A4), where William of Orange stayed in 1688 on his way to London, having been invited to 'invade' by Protestant nobles who were disenchanted with the Catholic King James II.

WALK 7
Hungerford, Freeman's Marsh and Standen Manor

Start/finish	Town Hall in the High Street, Hungerford (SU 337 685); parking (pay and display) in Church Street (SU 336 685) and Station Road (SU 339 685)
Alternative start/finish	Hungerford railway station (SU 340 685)
Distance	11.2km (7 miles); alternative start/finish: add 0.4km (¼ mile)
Total ascent	110m; alternative start/finish: add 0m
Time	3hr; alternative start/finish: add 0hr
Map	OS Explorer 158
Refreshments	Hungerford: lots of choice; Froxfield: the Pelican Inn (01488 682479, off route); Cobbs Farm Shop & Kitchen (01488 686770, off route)
Public transport	Trains to Hungerford; bus service to Hungerford from Newbury and Swindon (excluding Sundays)

From historic Hungerford, the walk heads westwards along the canal to Froxfield Bridge, from where a short detour leads to a pub and picturesque almshouses. The route then leaves the canal and heads past North Standen and the attractive red-brick Standen Manor, before heading back towards Hungerford. The final leg meanders through the wildlife-rich habitats of Freeman's Marsh and Hungerford Marsh nature reserves, straddling the River Dun.

Alternative start from the railway station
Exit the station from Platform 2 and turn right (west), then cross the road and follow the path signposted for the 'town centre and High Street' to reach the High Street. Turn left and then right across the road (A338) to the Town Hall (adds 200 metres each way).

The market town of **Hungerford**, which lies close to the western edge of Berkshire, is the only place

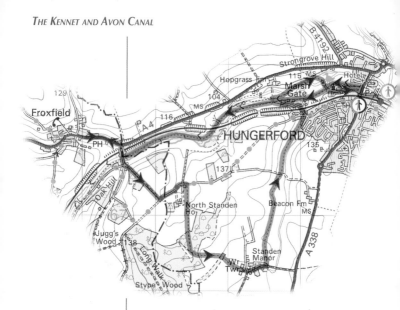

in the country that still holds the Hocktide Festival, the highlight of which is Tutti Day (second Tuesday after Easter), when the Hocktide Court is held and the Tutti Men visit every house with common rights. The present St Lawrence's Church dates from 1816; inside is the much mutilated effigy of Sir Robert de Hungerford (d.1352).

The Bear Hotel, about 200 metres north along the A338 at the junction with the A4, is where William of Orange met with King James II's commissioners in 1688 during the 'Glorious Revolution'. Shortly after this meeting, James II fled to France, which opened the way for William to rule jointly as William III with his wife, Mary II.

Stand with your back to Hungerford's Town Hall and turn left down the High Street, passing under the railway bridge. Just before the bridge over the canal, fork slightly left down beside the shops, passing the Tutti Pole tea shop, to reach the canal; this was once the site of Hungerford Wharf. Boat trips along the canal, on The Rose of Hungerford (01635 255367), operate from the opposite bank during the summer. ▶

Turn left along the towpath, soon passing the lock (74) to reach a swing bridge (85) beside St Lawrence's Church (left). Continue straight on along the towpath, passing through gates, to enter a field that forms part of Freeman's Marsh. Keep ahead past Hungerford Marsh Lock (73) with its swing bridge (86), before going through another gate and continuing to reach Cobblers Lock (72).

To visit **Cobbs Farm Shop & Kitchen**, cross the canal via the swing bridge at Hungerford Marsh Lock and turn left towards the house. Bear right along the track and cross the River Dun via the footbridge to reach the A4, with the shop opposite; retrace your steps back to the canal (650 metres each way).

Straight on across the bridge over the canal leads to the A4 and the Bear Hotel.

The former wharf site at Hungerford

Keep to the canalside path for 1.8km, passing a footbridge then going under the **railway bridge** to reach a minor road bridge (90) near **Froxfield**. After passing under the bridge, double back up to the minor road and turn right.

To visit Froxfield

Turn left (north) across the canal and follow the minor road over the railway to a T-junction. Turn left beside the A4 for 150 metres to the Pelican Inn; some 400 metres further along the road are the picturesque almshouses. These late 17th-century almshouses were built to house widows of clergymen and today still operate as a sheltered housing scheme for women. The 50 cottages are built as a quadrangle, with a cupola-topped gatehouse and central chapel.

The canal and Freeman's Marsh at Hungerford Marsh Lock (73)

Follow the minor road for 100 metres to a junction beside some houses at **Oak Hill** and bear left along the track. Keep ahead along the bridleway, heading uphill for 600

metres to a minor road, and then turn left for 400 metres. After passing a track (path) on the left, just after a house on the right, turn right (south) along the enclosed and signed path, passing to the left of **North Standen House**.

Keep along the fenced route between fields and then between trees, later following it as it bears left to enter a field. ▶ Keep ahead along the field margin, which is followed by a line of wooden pylons, towards some farm buildings. Continue along the track to a lane and go straight on (left) for 300 metres past some buildings at Standen Farm, following the lane slightly downhill. Immediately after the gated entrance on the left, turn left through a gate and head northwards through the field; over to the left is **Standen Manor**.

To the south-east is the broad outline of the North Hampshire Downs.

> The present-day red-brick **Standen Manor** was built in 1732, but the manor of South Standen dates back to before the Domesday Book. From the 12th century, it was held by the Hussey family and became known as Standen Hussey; by 1486, the manor belonged to Sir Reginald Bray, chief minister of King Henry VII, and later passed to the Goddard family, who held the manor for 150 years.

Leave through a gate and follow the right-hand field margin northwards through a long field. At the far right corner, bear diagonally right through the trees and continue northwards along the right-hand side of the next field. Where the boundary swings right, go straight on across the field, pass through the hedge and keep ahead through the next field to reach a minor road on the edge of **Hungerford**.

Cross straight over and follow Marsh Lane opposite, heading north-westwards (play area on right). Pass under the railway bridge, keep left along the lane to its end and go through the gate to enter Freeman's Marsh at **Marsh Gate**. Bear diagonally right to arrive at Hungerford Marsh Lock (passed earlier in the walk) and cross the swing bridge between the two lock gates to a signposted path junction. Turn right (north-east) across the common, cross a footbridge and continue north-eastwards to a fence, with the River Dun beyond.

Freeman's Marsh, owned by the Town and Manor of Hungerford, provides several important habitats supporting a rich wildlife. The River Dun, a typical chalk stream, is home to trout and bullheads, plants such as water crowfoot and yellow iris, and the endangered water vole; the wet meadows are home to southern marsh orchids and marsh marigolds. Birds include kingfishers and reed buntings.

In the 14th century, registered commoners were given the right to fish and graze animals on Freeman's Marsh and these rights are still exercised under the rules of the Hocktide Court.

Turn right and follow the fence on the left. Go through a gate, cross a footbridge over the river and keep ahead, soon passing a gate to enter Hungerford Marsh Nature Reserve, where a mix of water meadow and reedbed habitats support a rich variety of wildlife. Ignore a path to the left and follow the path as it bears right to pass some gates and a footbridge. Cross the canal via the swing bridge (85) and head through the churchyard, keeping left at the split and passing St Lawrence's Church.

Leave the churchyard through the gate and turn left along Church Lane, soon passing the grassy area known as The Croft. ◄ Keep straight on between buildings to reach the High Street and turn right to return to the Town Hall (or to return to the railway station, retrace the outward route).

Prior to medieval times, this was most likely the village green; the land was later given to the town by John Undewes in the 16th century 'to sport herein'.

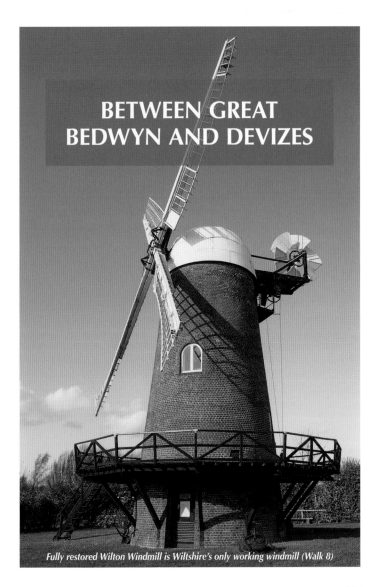

BETWEEN GREAT
BEDWYN AND DEVIZES

Fully restored Wilton Windmill is Wiltshire's only working windmill (Walk 8)

WALK 8
Great Bedwyn, Crofton and Wilton

Start/finish	Great Bedwyn railway station (SU 279 645); car park beside the canal (SU 280 644) south-east of the railway station or on-street parking in the village
Distance	9.5km (6 miles)
Total ascent	135m
Time	2½hr
Map	OS Explorer 157
Refreshments	Great Bedwyn: the Cross Keys (01672 870332), the Three Tuns (01672 870280), shop; Crofton Pumping Station: café (01672 870300); Wilton: the Swan (01672 870274)
Public transport	Trains to Great Bedwyn; bus services to Great Bedwyn from Marlborough and Hungerford (except Sundays)

From Great Bedwyn, known as Bedewinde in the Domesday Book, the walk follows the canal south-westwards to arrive at the world-famous Crofton Pumping Station, which houses two impressive steam-driven beam engines dating from the early 19th century. Then it's off alongside Wilton Water to reach the village of Wilton, before passing the picturesque Wilton Windmill. The final section heads through the wooded landscape of Bedwyn Brail and Wilton Brail, before following the canal back to Great Bedwyn.

At lock 61, a crossing track follows the course of a Roman road that ran between Venta Bulgarum (Winchester) and Cunetio (near Mildenhall).

From the railway station in Great Bedwyn, head south-west to the main road and turn left. After crossing the canal, turn right and head through the car park (SU 280 644) to join the towpath.

Follow the towpath south-westwards for 2.8km, passing four locks (64 to 61). ◄ Just before the fifth lock (60), the walk turns left to cross a footbridge beside the sluice-gate weir at **Wilton Water**. However, before that, take a short detour to visit **Crofton Pumping Station and Beam Engines**.

**To visit Crofton Pumping
Station and Beam Engines**

Turn right across the canal using
the lock gate (60) and follow the
path through the tunnel under the
railway, then up the steps. Having
visited the pumping station, retrace
your steps back to Wilton Water.

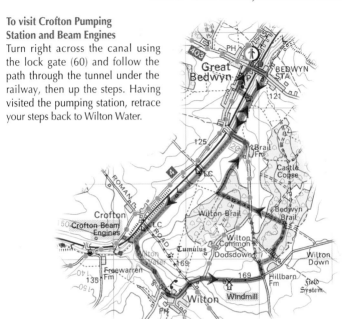

Located near the summit of the canal is the world-
famous **Crofton Pumping Station**. Built in 1807,
the pumps were used to raise water 12m from
natural springs at Wilton up to the summit of the
canal to replenish the water lost each time a boat
went through a lock. In response to increasing traffic along the canal, Wilton Water was created in
1836 to provide a larger store of water that could
be pumped into the canal. Although electric pumps
have been installed to pump water into the canal,
Crofton's magnificent steam-driven beam engines
– one of which (the Boulton and Watt engine dating from 1812) is the oldest working beam engine
in the world – are still used on several occasions
throughout the year (01672 870300).

The world-famous Crofton Pumping Station is well worth a short detour

Follow the path southwards alongside Wilton Water and then continue along the field edge to a path junction at the corner. Turn right and then left along the minor road through **Wilton**, with the pond on the right. At the junction, beside the Swan pub, keep left following the road uphill and ignore a road to the right. At the split, fork right (signposted to Shalbourne and windmill); after 400 metres there is an access track on the right for the **windmill** and picnic area.

The once derelict **Wilton Windmill**, which was built in 1821, has been lovingly restored to full working condition; the fantail keeps the sails aligned with the wind, acting as an automatic rudder (01672 870266).

Continue straight on along the road to the next junction (right) and turn left along the track for 200 metres. Go right and then bear right (signposted Great Bedwyn) to a gravel track. Turn left and follow the track (bridleway) through **Bedwyn Brail** for 500 metres to a grassy clearing and signed path junction beside a seat. ▶

Turn left (signposted for Wilton Road) and follow the wide grassy ride downhill. Go straight on through the field and cross over the minor road. Pass a gate and follow the track through the trees of **Wilton Brail**. Pass over the brow of the hill and head down to where the track curves left. Here, fork right on a path through the trees and enter a field.

Turn right and follow the right-hand edge through two fields. Once down in the bottom right corner, turn right through the trees to a minor road at **Brail Farm**. Turn left (north-west) along the minor road towards the canal at Mill Bridge (97).

Both Bedwyn Brail and Wilton Brail were once part of the extensive royal hunting ground of Savernake Forest.

The Swan pub in picturesque Wilton village

Fork left through the car park to the canal and turn right under the bridge. Follow the canal back towards **Great Bedwyn** and immediately after the lock (64), left over the bridge. With great care, go through gates either side of the railway and keep ahead through the field. Continue alongside the churchyard wall, with St Mary's Church on the right, to reach a road.

The **Church of St Mary the Virgin** dates from 1092, although most of what is visible dates from the 12th and 13th centuries. Step inside the rather large church to see an impressive monument to Sir John Seymour, father of Jane Seymour who married King Henry VIII in 1536, becoming his third wife; their son became Edward VI. (The Seymours lived at Wolfhall – passed on Walk 9 – and it was here that Jane Seymour met Henry VIII.)

The church also holds the stone figure of a knight, believed to be Sir Adam de Stokke (d.1313), and the tomb of Sir Roger de Stokke (d.1333), son of Sir Adam.

On the wall of the post office are some works by Lloyd's stonemason's yard (established 1790, closed 2009) who were involved with the construction of the canal.

Turn right along the road through **Great Bedwyn**, passing the post office, to a junction with the Cross Keys pub opposite; up to the left is the Three Tuns pub. ◄ Turn down to the right for 75 metres and then left back to the railway station, or continue across the two bridges back to the car park.

WALK 9
Wootton Rivers and Burbage

Start/finish	Canal bridge at Wootton Rivers (SU 198 629), 3.3km off the A346 between Marlborough and Burbage; small car park 50 metres north of the canal
Distance	12km (7½ miles)
Total ascent	105m
Time	3¼hr
Map	OS Explorer 157
Refreshments	Wootton Rivers: the Royal Oak (01672 810322); Burbage: the White Hart (01672 810336)
Public transport	Railway station at Great Bedwyn; bus services to Burbage (excluding Sunday) from Marlborough, Ludgershall and Great Bedwyn

The first part of the walk follows the canal eastwards, passing Burbage Wharf, with its replica crane, before briefly leaving the canal to pass over the Bruce Tunnel and then continuing to Wolfhall Bridge, following the summit pound (or highest section) of the canal. Here, the route leaves the canal and heads south to Wolfhall – once home to Jane Seymour, who married Henry VIII – before heading to Burbage. The final section meanders north-westwards through fields with views of the Pewsey Downs before dropping back down to Wootton Rivers.

From the canal bridge (108), with the village behind you, turn left along the towpath (canal on left) past the lock (51); the walk follows the canal eastwards for 5.1km. However, a quick visit to Wootton Rivers is worth the short detour: 100 metres north along the main street, on the left, is St Andrew's Church, and 250 metres further on is the thatch-roofed Royal Oak (right); retrace your steps and turn left along the towpath.

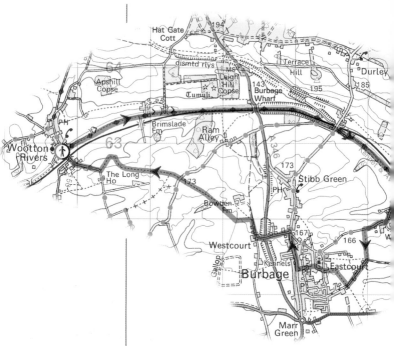

Wootton Rivers,
first recorded in AD804,
gained part of its name from the de la Rivière
family, who held the manor from the early 13th
century. In 1441 the manor was sold to Sir John
Seymour of Savernake and then passed through
a succession of Seymours and Dukes of Somerset
until 1692, when it was bequeathed to St John's
College, Cambridge.

The small 14th-century St Andrew's Church has
a picturesque wooden steeple and a clock made by
local man John Spratt to commemorate George V's
coronation in 1911. The clock was made from scrap
metal and on one face the numbers have been
replaced with the words 'Glory be to God'.

Follow the canal past lock 52, then **Brimslade Farm** and lock (53) and then past Cadley Lock (54) to reach **Burbage Wharf**; the section between Cadley Lock and Crofton Top Lock (55) forms the summit pound of the canal (level section between locks); the railway running parallel, just on the right, is the line from London to the south-west.

Burbage Wharf was built in 1831 to allow the transportation of timber and locally made bricks. The reconstructed timber wharfside crane (private) rotates around a central pillar, or king post, with a large stone counterweight, and was capable of lifting 2 tons; these cranes were once a common sight along the canal.

Just to the north is **Savernake Forest**, a remnant of a medieval royal hunting ground. William the Conqueror gave Savernake to one of his knights, and it has passed in an unbroken line for over 30 generations. Although privately owned, it has been leased to the Forestry Commission and walkers can explore most of the forest.

The canalside path takes you past Burbage Wharf

Narrowboat emerging from the eastern end of the Bruce Tunnel

Pass under the road bridge (A346) and continue for 900 metres to reach the Bruce Tunnel.

The 459-metre-long **Bruce Tunnel**, the only long tunnel along the canal, is named after Thomas Brudenell-Bruce, Earl of Ailesbury, who owned the land through which the canal passed (the family still own Savernake Forest). The tunnel has no towpath, which meant that the horse-drawn barges had to be pulled through the tunnel by the boatmen using chains fixed to the walls, while the horses were taken over the top.

Bear right uphill, passing under the railway, and continue along the enclosed path to a minor road, with the former Forest Hotel (private) on the right. Cross straight over and take the driveway opposite to its end. Keep ahead along the path and turn left down the steps back to the canal beside the tunnel; turn right. Continue eastwards along the towpath for 1.1km to the next bridge (Wolfhall Bridge, 103). Leave the canal here and turn right along the track heading up to **Wolfhall**. At the farm, turn right along the lane for 300 metres.

Mentioned in the Domesday Book as Ulfela, **Wolfhall** became noted as the home of the Seymour family, especially Sir John and Lady Margaret. Their daughter Jane married Henry VIII as his third queen and gave him a son (Edward VI); Henry VIII visited Wolfhall in 1535 and 1539. (There is an impressive memorial to Sir John Seymour in the Church of St Mary the Virgin at Great Bedwyn, which is visited in Walk 8.)

The great manor has long since disappeared, although it probably stood in the field between the present Victorian Wolfhall Manor (hidden by trees) and the brick cottage that lies just to the north, easily recognisable by its tall Tudor chimneys.

Turn left along a signposted path, following the left-hand field edge. Just before the field corner, dogleg left into the adjacent field and keep ahead to a junction with a track. Go straight on (south-west) along the track for 450 metres, passing some cottages and ignoring a bridleway to the right. At the slight right-hand bend, turn right past a gate and follow the path along the right-hand side of the cricket ground and then along the right-hand field edge. Turn left at the corner, still following the right-hand field edge for 50 metres, then keep ahead through the trees. Follow the driveway to a lane in **Eastcourt** (125 metres to the left is the village hall and car park).

Cross slightly right and follow the lane (Eastcourt) opposite, passing just south of All Saints Church. Where the lane swings right, go straight on along the enclosed path. Cross straight over the road and follow another enclosed path between houses to reach the High Street in **Burbage** beside a picturesque thatched cottage (the Old Nursery) and turn right.

Burbage has a number of lovely thatched and timber-framed cottages

Burbage stands on the watershed at the eastern end of the Vale of Pewsey; streams draining to the west join the Salisbury Avon, while streams to the east drain via the Rivers Dun and Kennet to join the River Thames. The village is formed of three old linear settlements that grew along three separate streets; Eastcourt, Westcourt and the area along the High Street.

    Eastcourt is home to a small green, some thatched and timber-framed 17th- and 18th-century cottages, and the village church. All Saints Church, which stands on the site of an earlier Saxon church mentioned in the Domesday Book, was largely rebuilt in the 1850s, with the exception of the 14th-century tower. The smaller hamlet of Westcourt lies to the west of the A346.

Follow the High Street northwards for 500 metres, passing the White Hart pub, to a junction on the left (taking care at sections without pavement). Some 600 metres north along the High Street is Stibb Green and the Three Horseshoes pub (01672 810324). Turn left along the road towards **Westcourt**, crossing the bridge over the **A346** to a T-junction. Turn right for 250 metres; after the last building on the left, turn left along a permissive path running beside the field edge and then keep ahead across the field (the right of way on the map heads north-west across the field, passing **Bowden Farm**). Go through into the next field and bear slightly right (north-west) across the field to the lower corner near some trees. Keep ahead into the next field and continue in the same direction to a stile on the far side. Continue across a third field to a gap in the hedge. Cross over the lane, pass a gate and follow the left-hand boundary for 175 metres. Dogleg left into the adjacent field and keep ahead with the field edge on the right; ahead are views towards Martinsell Hill (visited on Walk 10).

Keep alongside the right-hand field edge as it bears right and then swings left at the corner, to reach a gate on the western edge of the field. Exit the field and turn right down the lane towards **Wootton Rivers**. Keep right (straight on) at the junction, crossing the bridge over the railway, back to the canal.

From Burbage the route heads through fields on its way back to Wootton Rivers

WALK 10

Pewsey Wharf, Martinsell Hill and Oare Hill

Start/finish	Pewsey Wharf (pay-and-display car park) on the A345 beside the canal bridge (SU 157 610), 1.2km north of Pewsey
Alternative start/finish	Pewsey railway station (SU 160 604)
Distance	10.5km (6½ miles); alternative start/finish: add 1.6km (1 mile)
Total ascent	230m; alternative start/finish: add 20m
Time	3hr; alternative start/finish: add ½hr
Map	OS Explorer 157
Refreshments	Pewsey Wharf: the Waterfront (01672 564020)
Public transport	Trains to Pewsey station (alternative start only); bus services to Pewsey Wharf from Salisbury and Swindon (excluding Sundays)

A hilly route with some fantastic views across the Vale of Pewsey, described by William Cobbett in his *Rural Rides* (where it is known as 'Valley of Avon') as 'a most beautiful sight'. From Pewsey Wharf, the walk heads eastwards along the canal before heading north to pass West Wick Farm and then climbing up to the crest of the chalk downs. Admire the views as the walk loops around Martinsell Hill – site of an Iron Age hill fort – before heading off to Oare Hill. Take time to soak up more views stretching out to the south, west and north – including the Georgian Rainscombe House – before heading steeply down to the valley and then following the canal back to the start.

Alternative start from Pewsey station

Leave from Platform 2, head down the access road, cross over the main road (A345) and turn left along the pavement for 750 metres to reach Pewsey Wharf.

From Pewsey Wharf, walk eastwards alongside the canal for 2km, passing Pains Bridge (113); the return route comes across the bridge. Just before the next bridge (112), fork right up to the minor road and turn left across the canal. Follow the road northwards, keeping ahead at the junction. Pass some houses (right) and continue up the tarmac drive towards **West Wick Farm** and West Wick House. Then keep ahead along the grassy bridleway and go through a gate to a Y-junction.

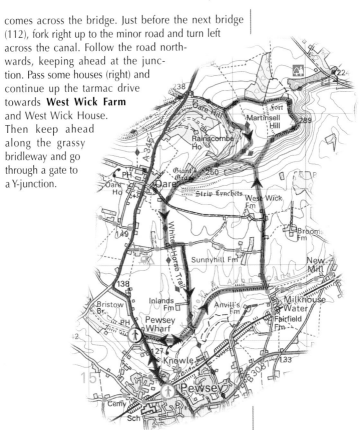

Fork right (signposted Martinsell Hill) and follow the route curving up the slope. ▶ At the top of the rise, bear right alongside the fence and turn left through a gate to enter a field. Turn right to the field corner (path junction) and keep ahead along the narrow path past trees to reach a seat with a great view, beside the ditch and rampart earthworks of the former Iron Age hill fort crowning **Martinsell Hill**.

To miss out Martinsell Hill, take the left-hand fork, signposted to Clench Common and Oare Hill (minus 2.7km).

Keep ahead through the gate and follow the level route as it curves left (north), with old beech trees on the right. Keep beside the fence on the left to a fence corner and turn left, still following the fence on the left. Go through a gate and continue to a signposted cross-junction at Withy Copse.

Go straight on along a tree-shaded route, ignoring a crossing path (note that the right of way on the map heads south across the field from SU 171 641 to SU 172 638). Keep ahead to a track and turn left following the White Horse Trail (permissive route) into the field; bear right alongside the fence for 850 metres as it swings left and right (official right of way rejoins here) to reach a stile and gate in the south-west corner. ◄

The shorter route missing out Martinsell Hill rejoins here.

Cross the stile and follow the **White Horse Trail** and Mid-Wilts Way (MWW), keeping the fence on your right and soon passing through the earthworks of the **Giant's Grave** to reach a **trig point**. The earthworks are the remains of an Iron Age promontory

The view looking east from Martinsell Hill

156

hill fort or settlement, protected on its eastern edge by a single rampart and ditch.

Heading along Oare Hill towards the earthworks of the Giant's Grave

Having admired the views, head steeply downhill, following the fence on the right. Cross a stile in the bottom right corner and continue across the field to a track (400 metres to the right is **Oare**). Cross straight over into the field opposite and follow the right-hand margin for 500 metres to a lane.

Turn left along the lane for 200 metres, then right along the track (bridleway) to cross the canal via Pains Bridge (113), passed earlier in the walk; the gate ahead on the left gives access to Jones's Mill Nature Reserve (Wiltshire Wildlife Trust).

Jones's Mill Nature Reserve is the only fenland or wetland reserve in Wiltshire. The site was previously used as a traditional water meadow that was allowed to flood with mineral-rich spring-fed waters during the winter to produce an early growth of grass in the spring.

After crossing Pains Bridge, immediately turn left and then left again to go under the bridge and retrace the outward route, heading west, back to **Pewsey Wharf**.

WALK 11
Wilcot and Woodborough

Start/finish	The Golden Swan, Wilcot (SU 143 611), 2km north-west of Pewsey; limited on-street parking in the village
Distance	9.7km (6 miles)
Total ascent	125m
Time	2¾hr
Map	OS Explorer 157 and 130
Refreshments	Wilcot: the Golden Swan (01672 562289); Woodborough Garden Centre: café (01672 852114, off route)
Public transport	Limited service between Devizes and Pewsey to Wilcot (except Sundays); or follow canal east for 1.9km each way to Pewsey Wharf (A345) for buses between Swindon and Salisbury (except Sundays)

From picturesque Wilcot, with its pub and thatched cottages, the walk heads west along the canal before taking a short loop up Woodborough Hill for a great panoramic view. It then meanders through Woodborough, another peaceful and picturesque village, before heading across fields back to Wilcot, passing the historic Swanborough Tump on the way.

Wilcot is in two parts: the area around the church, and a linear settlement to the north along the main road that crosses the canal. The manor of Wilcot was mentioned in the Domesday Book, when it was held by Edward of Salisbury; the family gave the manor to Bradenstoke Priory and they held it until Henry VIII's Dissolution of the Monasteries. The present manor house, with its 17th-century circular thatched dovecote, is probably built on the site of the original manor. Nearby is the Church of the Holy Cross (passed at the end of the walk) which dates from the late 12th century, although there have been numerous changes over the centuries.

Stand facing the Golden Swan pub in Wilcot and turn right (south-west) along the lane, with thatched cottages on the right. At the left-hand bend, turn right along the track, with houses on the left and a recreation ground on the right. Join the main road beside the war memorial and bear left. After crossing the canal, turn left down to the towpath and follow the canal westwards, passing under a bridge (119) and then passing Wide Water to reach Lady's Bridge (120); over to the right is the cone-shaped **Picked Hill**. ▸

The track to the south heads directly to the Swanborough Tump.

> The rather ornate **Lady's Bridge**, with stone balustrade, and the widened section of canal – known as Wide Water – were built to form a landscaped lake setting as a favour to the local landowner, Lady Susannah Wroughton, in return for allowing the canal to be built across her land.

Keep ahead along the towpath for 1.5km to the next bridge (122), where the walk leaves the canal; the 145km (90 mile) **White Horse Trail**, which visits all eight white horse hill figures within Wiltshire, follows the canal along this section.

From the bridge, turn right along the track, keeping ahead at some

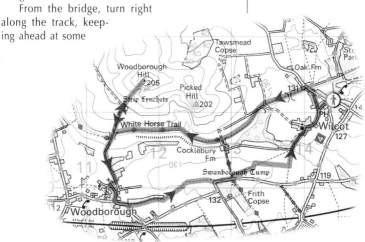

barns. Go through a gate and climb more steeply past some trees to reach the top of **Woodborough Hill**; from here there are extensive views south to Salisbury Plain, north-east to Martinsell Hill (visited in Walk 10) and north-west to Milk Hill (highest point in Wiltshire) and the Alton Barnes White Horse (visited in Walk 12).

Retrace your steps back to the bridge and go straight across the canal. Follow the track south towards **Woodborough**, passing Church Farm; opposite the farm, a squeeze stile on the right gives access to St Mary Magdalene Church. Once past the farm, follow the lane to the right, then turn left to a T-junction, with thatched cottages on the right.

Woodborough, like its neighbour Wilcot, has a number of picturesque thatched cottages and a church. Originally built in the 13th century, St Mary Magdalene Church was mostly rebuilt in 1850.

During the early 20th century, Walter T Ware grew large numbers of daffodils and tulips at Nursery Farm (now Woodborough Garden Centre,

The ornate Lady's Bridge over the Kennet and Avon Canal

The walk passes through picturesque Woodborough, with its lovely thatched cottages

with café and farm shop) to sell in London's Covent Garden; Ware also cultivated the *Narcissus* 'Fortune' (daffodil) that is still widely grown today.

Turn left and where the road swings hard right, go straight on through the gate. ▶ Follow the left-hand field edge, go through a gate in the corner and follow the enclosed track, later doglegging left and keeping ahead through trees before entering a field.

Continue straight on through several fields, following the left-hand edge to join a lane. Bear left (straight on) along the lane for 275 metres to an entrance on the left; on the right (south side of the road), just on the edge of Frith Copse and marked by a sarsen stone, is the **Swanborough Tump**. ▶

Turn left onto the tarmac drive and immediately turn right over a stile. Head diagonally left (north-east) across the field and cross stiles at the corner. Turn left along the field edge for 40 metres, then turn right along the grassy strip between the fields to a track and turn left to the field edge (on the map the right of way heads diagonally north-east across the fields). Leave the field over a stile beside the gate. Bear right along the track (this later becomes a lane) to reach a junction in **Wilcot**, with the Church of the Holy Cross and Wilcot Manor on the left. Turn right along the lane back to the start.

For the café, follow the road south-east for 350 metres to a junction and fork left (Manningford) for 100 metres to the garden centre on the left (retrace steps).

A plaque commemorates the meeting here between Alfred the Great and his brother Ethelred on their way to fight the invading Danes in AD871.

WALK 12

Honeystreet and the Alton Barnes White Horse

Start/finish	Car park on the south side of All Cannings Bridge (127) just north of All Cannings village (SU 076 622)
Alternative start/finish	Car park near Knap Hill (SU 115 638), 1.9km north of Alton Barnes
Distance	12.1km (7½ miles); alternative start/finish: add 1.1km (¾ mile)
Total ascent	255m; alternative start/finish: add 30m
Time	3¾hr; alternative start/finish: add ½hr
Map	OS Explorer 157
Refreshments	All Cannings: the King's Arms (01380 860328, off route); Honeystreet: the Barge Inn (01672 851705), Honeystreet Café (01672 851232)
Public transport	Limited bookable bus service between Devizes and Pewsey stops at Honeystreet (excluding Sundays)

From All Cannings Bridge, the walk follows the canal eastwards as far as Honeystreet, passing the canalside Barge Inn on the way. The canal is then left behind in favour of the neighbouring villages of Alton Barnes and Alton Priors, before the walk heads up onto the rolling chalk downs to visit the Alton Barnes White Horse. After contouring round Milk Hill, Wiltshire's highest hill, the route briefly meets up with the impressive Saxon earthworks of the Wansdyke. Admire the views from this lofty location before heading back down to the canal.

Alternative start

From the car park near Knap Hill, cross over the road, go through a gate and immediately left through another gate. Follow the permissive path southwards through the field. Go through a gate on the right and bear half-left (south-west) up **Walkers Hill**, passing through a gate on the way, to reach a col (SU 111 635) just to the right of **Adam's Grave**. Turn right to follow the main walk; this point is

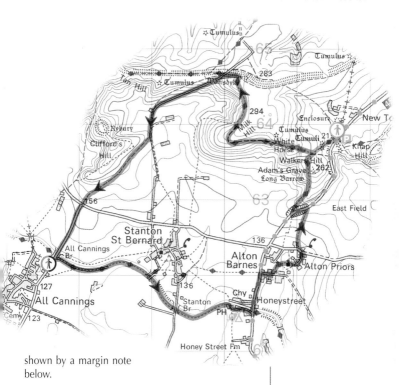

shown by a margin note below.

Exit the back of the car park and turn right along the towpath, following the canal eastwards for 3.1km to **Honeystreet**, passing two bridges and then the canal-side Barge Inn on the way. Just before the next bridge (124), fork right up to the road and turn left across the canal; on the right is the Honeystreet Café and wharf. Follow the minor road northwards for 500 metres towards **Alton Barnes**. ▶

At the junction, turn right along the lane signposted for the church; shortly before reaching the church, fork left through a wooden turnstile. To visit St Mary's Church,

After 275 metres, the field entrance on the left gives access to a memorial on the last remaining air-raid shelter (SU 104 617) from the former World War II RAF Alton Barnes.

The church dates from Saxon times. Call in to see the 16th-century tie-beamed and wind-braced roof, a Georgian gallery and some interesting monuments.

keep ahead along the lane for 75 metres to a gate on the left. ◄

From the wooden turnstile, follow the cobbled path diagonally through the field (north-east), keeping ahead at a crossing cobbled path. Go through turnstiles either side of footbridges in the trees and keep to the cobbled path, ignoring another crossing path and passing just left of All Saints Church in neighbouring **Alton Priors**.

Step inside the Norman **All Saints Church**, cared for by the Churches Conservation Trust, to see some fine Jacobean carved wooden choir stalls, a tomb chest to William Button (d.1590) and two sarsen stones hidden under trapdoors in the floor. These may be from an earlier sacred site – early Christian churches were sometimes built on existing religious sites. Outside in the churchyard stands an ancient yew tree (another pagan symbol), said to be well over a thousand years old.

Following the cobbled path between the churches at Alton Barnes and Alton Priors

Leave the field through a wooden turnstile and follow the lane through the village to a junction beside a large thatched barn (spot the white horse carved on the sarsen stone on the small green). Turn left for a few metres and then turn right along the tarmac track (signposted 'bridleway only'). At its end, continue straight on up the shrub-shaded bridleway to reach a road.

With care, turn left down the road for 250 metres to the left-hand bend, and turn sharp right up the signposted path to a gate beside information boards for the White Horse Trail and Pewsey Downs National Nature Reserve. Go through the gate and follow the prominent grassy path straight on up **Walkers Hill**; from the path you can see the white horse that the route soon passes. (Alternatively, for a shorter section on the road, turn right up the road for 100 metres, turn left over a stile, then head north-westwards steeply uphill (open access land) to reach the prominent path just over the brow of the ridge; turn right.)

Following the canal past the Barge Inn at Honeystreet

The path passes the Alton Barnes White Horse

The **Pewsey Downs National Nature Reserve** covers a large expanse of chalk grassland that is home to several varieties of orchid and a range of butterflies, including marble white and chalkhill blue. The 145km (90 mile) **White Horse Trail** visits all eight white horse hill figures within Wiltshire.

The route from the alternative start/finish point joins the walk here and turns right.

The path skirts to the left of the summit, which is crowned by the prominent hump of **Adam's Grave** (the remains of a Neolithic burial mound), to reach a junction of routes at a col. ◀ Bear half-left, following the level path (the White Horse Trail and the Mid-Wilts Way) as it contours round the hill to pass just above the **Alton Barnes White Horse** (commissioned by Robert Pile in 1812). Admire the views south across the Vale of Pewsey to the distant Salisbury Plain.

Keep ahead (west), go through a gate and continue to contour round **Milk Hill** as the path swings right (northwards). ▸ Go through a gate and follow the fence on the right, passing another gate, with extensive views to the left (west) including the earthworks of Rybury hill fort (an Iron Age hill fort overlying an earlier Neolithic causewayed camp); along here there are a number of sarsen stones lying on the ground (see 'Geology' section in the Introduction). Turn right through a gate and follow the right-hand fence northwards through the field to leave through another gate.

Turn left down the track with the **Wansdyke** on the right; this massive linear earthwork, dating from Saxon times (late 5th century), stretches east–west across the Marlborough Downs above the Vale of Pewsey from Marlborough to Morgan's Hill (a longer section of the Wansdyke is followed on Walk 13). Views ahead include Tan Hill and the meandering outline of the Wansdyke, slightly right is the distant Lansdowne Monument, with the cone-shaped Silbury Hill and the Marlborough Downs to the north.

At the track junction, turn left down the track for 1.5km, passing a barn (right) on the way, to reach a junction 400 metres after the barn. Leave the main track here and fork right along the enclosed bridleway, heading south-westwards for 1.3km to reach a road junction at Cannings Cross. Go straight over and follow the minor road downhill for 750 metres to **All Cannings Bridge** over the canal. Continue along the road for a further 100 metres and turn sharp left, doubling back along the track to the car park beside the canal. ▸

At 295m, Milk Hill is the highest point in Wiltshire and Britain's second highest chalk hill.

Off route in All Cannings is the King's Arms pub and the 13th-century All Saints Church.

WALK 13

All Cannings, the Wansdyke and Bishops Cannings

Start/finish	Car park on the south side of All Cannings Bridge (127) just north of All Cannings (SU 076 622)
Distance	14.5km (9 miles)
Total ascent	250m
Time	4¼hr
Map	OS Explorer 157
Refreshments	All Cannings: the King's Arms (01380 860328, off route); Bishops Cannings: the Crown Inn (01380 860218)
Public transport	Daily bus services to Bishops Cannings from Swindon and Devizes
Note	If using public transport, start the walk from Bishops Cannings (SU 037 641).

A great day walk starting out from All Cannings in the Vale of Pewsey, to the east of Devizes. The route heads north and climbs to the top of the Pewsey Downs, then turns westwards to follow a lovely sweeping stretch of the Saxon earthworks of the Wansdyke, offering some great views, before heading back down into the vale to visit Bishops Cannings. The final section follows the canal eastwards back to the start.

The track to the left leads to All Cannings, home to the King's Arms pub and 13th-century All Saints Church (some 900 metres each way).

Exit from the back of the car park at All Cannings Bridge (127) and turn left (west) along the canal for 400 metres, passing under the bridge. At the next bridge (128), leave the towpath and turn right across the canal. ◄

Once across the bridge, immediately fork right following the grassy strip across the field towards the buildings at **Cannings Cross Farm**. Over to the left, near the field edge, is the **Long Barrow**. This modern Neolithic-style columbarium (for housing cremated remains) was built in 2014.

Looking west along the giant Saxon earthworks of the Wansdyke

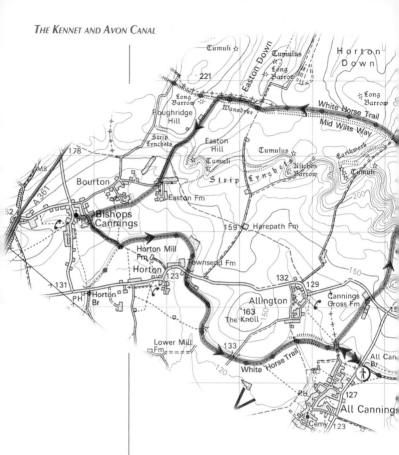

Continue along the track, cross over the road and keep ahead up to two gates side-by-side. Go through the left-hand gate, follow the enclosed bridleway and then keep ahead across the field. Leave through a gate and continue uphill for 850 metres, below and to the left of the remains of **Rybury hill fort** that crown **Clifford's Hill**, and passing through a gate to reach another gate near the top.

Go through the gate and follow the fence on the left over **Tan Hill** to reach the earthworks of the **Wansdyke** at the field corner. Go through a gate and turn left down the track to a T-junction. Turn left and then immediately right through a gate to follow the **White Horse Trail**, **Mid-Wilts Way** and **Wansdyke Path** along the impressive earthwork for 2.5km as it sweeps along the downs, offering some great views. Go through several gates, ignore all crossing routes and pass to the right of some barns near the halfway point. The view includes Morgan's Hill with its twin masts ahead (west-north-west), Cherhill Down and the Lansdowne Monument slightly right (north-north-west), and the Marlborough Downs including Silbury Hill to the far right (north-north-east).

The **Wansdyke**, a massive linear earthwork dating from Saxon times (late 5th century), stretches west across the Marlborough Downs above the Vale of Pewsey from Marlborough to Morgan's Hill; the earthwork is probably named after the Saxon god Woden. As for its purpose, opinion is divided; it could have been a defensive structure to stop West Saxons encroaching from the upper Thames Valley, or maybe its purpose was one of demarking territorial areas.

The 145km (90 mile) White Horse Trail visits all eight white horse hill figures within Wiltshire; the Mid-Wilts Way stretches for 109km (68 miles) across Wiltshire from Ham to Mere; and the 21km (13 mile) Wansdyke Path heads west from Marlborough to Morgan's Hill.

Go through a gate to join a well-defined farm track (SU 057 657) and turn left, passing a barn (right) after 300 metres. Continue downhill to a junction of tracks at **Easton Farm**. Turn right for a few metres, then go left through a gate and head diagonally right (south-west) across paddocks separated by gates. ▶

An alternative permissive route follows the lane for 300 metres and then turns left alongside the hedge and fence before turning right along the right of way, following the field edge.

171

Continue along the left-hand field edge, go through a gate and cross the footbridge. Keep ahead through the narrow field and cross another footbridge to enter a large field. Follow the right-hand field boundary to a crossing path (thatched cottage on the right) and keep ahead (slightly left), aiming for the church spire.

At the far side of the field, cross a footbridge and continue through the next field, following the right-hand margin. At the field corner, dogleg right through a gate and continue along the surfaced track to a lane (The Street) in **Bishops Cannings**.

The walk goes left here; however, to visit the pub and/or church, cross straight over and follow Church Walk past cottages and then through the churchyard,

The tall spire of St Mary's Church, Bishops Cannings, can be seen from miles around

172

The rare 17th-century penitent's pew inside St Mary's Church, Bishops Cannings

with St Mary's Church on the right, to reach Chandlers Lane, with the Crown Inn on the left. ▶ Retrace your steps along Church Walk back to the lane and turn right.

This is an alternative start/finish point for the walk if you are using public transport.

The village of **Bishops Cannings**, which dates back to before the Domesday Book, is dominated by the rather tall 15th-century spire of St Mary's Church – a local landmark that is visible from miles around. Step inside the church to see the finely carved, late 19th-century pew ends – each one is different – and take a look at the rare 17th-century penitent's pew. This is where local parishioners would sit beneath the large painted hand – the 'hand of God' or 'hand of meditation', with warnings about vanity, mortality and sin – while they pondered their sins.

Follow the lane for 75 metres and at the entrance to Court Farm, keep ahead (slightly left) along the track for 500 metres to the canal. Cross the swing bridge (133) and turn left along the canal towpath for 4.9km back to **All Cannings Bridge** (127).

WALK 14
Devizes, Caen Hill and Rowde

Start/finish	The Wharf, Devizes (SU 004 617); pay-and-display car park in Wharf Street accessed from the A361
Distance	10.5km (6½ miles)
Total ascent	110m
Time	3hr
Map	OS Explorer 156 and 157
Refreshments	Devizes: several choices, including Devizes Wharf Café (01380 721279), the Black Horse (01380 723930), Caen Hill Café (01380 724880); Rowde: the George and Dragon (01380 723053), the Cross Keys (01380 739567), shop
Public transport	Daily bus services to Devizes from Bath and Swindon, and from Trowbridge (excluding Sundays)

From Devizes Wharf, the walk heads west to follow the canal down the world-famous Caen Hill flight of locks before leaving the canal and heading north. After exploring the village of Rowde, the route heads back to the canal and follows a path up the north side of the Caen Hill pounds before retracing the outward route back to the wharf. Interesting diversions in Devizes include Wadworth's Brewery and the Wiltshire Heritage Museum.

The market town of **Devizes** (Thursday market) is home to a number of historic buildings including two churches (St Mary and St John) dating back to Norman times. From St John's Church you can see the present Devizes Castle (private), which was built by the Victorians on the site of a former Norman stronghold. To the north-west of the Market Place is Wadworth's Brewery (01380 732277), founded by Henry Alfred Wadworth in 1875; call in to learn more about their brewing heritage. To the south of the Market Place is the Wiltshire Heritage

Museum (01380 727369), which traces the history of Wiltshire over the last 6000 years. Devizes Wharf is home to the Kennet & Avon Canal Trust, a small museum and a café; during the summer there are boat trips along the canal from here.

Looking back up the impressive Caen Hill flight of locks

Exit the wharf in Devizes via the entrance beside the southern end of the long timber-balconied building (which houses the museum and café) and turn left along Couch Lane. Immediately after crossing the bridge, turn left down the path signposted for Caen Hill Locks. Follow the north side of the canal (soon, over to the left, is Wadworth's Brewery) and pass a lock (50) to join the main road (**A361**).

Do not cross the road but turn left across the canal and immediately turn left, then left again to head under the bridge. Follow the south side of the canal past three locks (across the canal, between the second lock (48) and the third (47), is the Black Horse pub), then head under the A361 again. Continue past two locks to reach the Sir Hugh Stockwell Lock (44), named after the former chairman of the Kennet & Avon Canal Trust, at the top of the magnificent central section of the **Caen Hill Locks** (44 through to 29); across the bridge is the Caen Hill Café.

Designed by John Rennie, the 16 locks of **Caen Hill Locks** were the last part of the canal to be completed. They form the middle group of 29 locks that cover a rise/fall of 72m in 3.3km from Devizes to Lower Foxhangers. Due to the steepness of the terrain along the Caen Hill flight of locks (lock 44 through to 29), the pounds had to be very short so they were extended sideways to allow enough water to be stored to operate each lock.

Head downhill beside the flight of locks; after passing lock 28, go under the road bridge (**B3101**). Continue past locks 27 to 23 in quick succession to a footbridge (145) beside the lock. Turn right across the canal here and then turn right again to start following the opposite bank of the canal back towards Devizes. After 150 metres, bear half-left down to a footbridge and stile. Cross over and follow the left-hand field margin. Go through a gate at the corner and continue along the hedge-lined track towards **Rowde**.

After 600 metres, follow the track as it turns left and at the road junction turn right along Rowde Court Road for 150 metres. Just after the small cul-de-sac on the left, turn

left along the tarmac path and then continue through the churchyard, passing to the left of St Matthew's Church. Follow the narrow path between buildings to join Cock Road beside a junction.

Heading back to Devizes Wharf

> There was a church in **Rowde** at the time of the Domesday Book; however, the present St Matthew's Church is more recent, mostly dating from Victorian rebuilding, although its tall tower is 15th century. Parts of the George and Dragon pub also date from the 15th century, although most buildings, such as the red-brick Rowde Hall with its stone facade, date from the 18th and 19th centuries. The architect and art historian Sir Matthew Digby Wyatt, who helped design Paddington station in London, was born in the village.

Turn right and follow the main street (A342) past the George and Dragon pub; just after the Cross Keys pub, turn right along Marsh Lane (**B3101**) past the shop,

177

The lane to the left leads up to Caen Hill car park and can be used instead of the Marsh Lane path.

keeping to the pavement on the left. At the edge of the village, keep ahead along the roadside path and as the road starts to curve right, take the option of the permissive path rather than following the pavement. Fork left through a gate into the field, where the path splits; turn right to follow the permissive path along the right-hand field edge, signposted for the locks. Pass through a gate and keep ahead through the next field before leaving to join a lane. ◄

Cross straight over and go through a gate opposite, following a footpath signposted 'Marsh Lane Footpath – bottom of locks' alongside the right-hand boundary. At the far right corner, leave the field and continue along the roadside path. Just before the canal bridge, turn left and cross the canal via the footbridge beside lock 28 (passed earlier); from here, there is a great view eastwards back up the flight of locks. Turn left along the towpath to lock 29 and turn left across the footbridge.

Keep ahead along the grassy path to the trees and turn right, heading uphill, keeping the rectangular lock pounds on the right (later a path from the access road passed earlier joins from the left). Once level with the car park (left), turn right between the pounds and cross the canal via the footbridge at lock 42. Turn left uphill, passing the Caen Hill Café, and retrace the outward route for 1.9km back to the wharf in **Devizes**.

Detour to Devizes town centre

To explore the town, leave the canal at bridge 141 and follow the A361 towards the town centre. At the mini-roundabout, beside Wadworth's Brewery, keep right (straight on) along Northgate Street to the Market Place and keep left. Just after the Swan Hotel (left), turn left along Snuff Street, cross over New Park Street (A361) and follow Couch Lane back to the wharf. For the museum, head south from the Market Place, following St John's Street and then Long Street past St John's Church to the museum; retrace your steps.

BETWEEN SEEND AND BRISTOL

Crossing the Avoncliff Aqueduct (Walks 16 and 17)

WALK 15
Seend and Seend Cleeve

Start/finish	Village hall and recreation ground parking area along Rusty Lane in Seend, just off the A361 (ST 943 611)
Distance	9.2km (5¾ miles)
Total ascent	120m
Time	2½hr
Map	OS Explorer 156
Refreshments	Seend Cleeve: the Barge Inn (01380 828230), the Brewery Inn (01380 828463, off route); Seend: the Bell Inn (01380 828338) and shop (both off route)
Public transport	Bus services to Seend from Swindon, Devizes and Trowbridge (excluding Sundays)
Note	The walk may also be started from Seend Wharf Bridge (ST 932 613) on minor road between the A365 and Seend Cleeve; limited roadside parking.

An easy figure-of-eight walk to the south-east of Melksham. From Seend the route heads downs through fields that were once home to the 19th-century Seend Ironworks to reach Seend Wharf and the Barge Inn. The route then heads up through Seend Cleeve before heading west to cross Semington Brook and arrive at picturesque Seend Park Farm with its lovely replica Wiltshire barn. From here, the route follows the canal past five locks before heading up to the ridge-top village of Seend. The final section takes you past the Holy Cross Church in Seend before heading back to the start.

Head north along Rusty Lane to a five-way junction and turn left along the enclosed bridleway (signposted Bollands Hill ½ mile), with views to the right.

At the junction, bear left along the track, which soon curves right to a lane (School Road). Turn right to a T-junction. Cross over the road and turn right along the pavement for 250 metres to a junction. Fork left along Pelch Lane for 10 metres and turn right over a stile. Head

northwards through the field, go anti-clockwise round the beech copse and head north-westwards down across the field. Cross a stile and follow the left-hand fence downhill; this area was once the site of Seend Ironworks.

The canalside Barge Inn at Seend Cleeve

The 17th-century antiquarian John Aubrey noted that the ironstone at Seend was 'the richest ever seen'; but although it may have been smelted locally

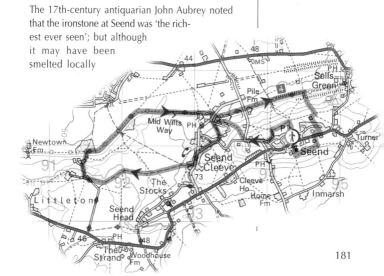

The walk skirts round the modern Wiltshire barn at Seend Park Farm

since the Iron Age, it was not until the 1850s that the iron ore was commercially quarried. Originally the ore was sent, via the canal, to Wales for smelting, until the **Seend Ironworks** were opened here, with three 15m-high blast furnaces. A tramway connected the works to the branch line running from Devizes to the main railway line near Trowbridge (the branch line closed in 1966). Between 1855 and 1871, 77,000 tonnes of iron ore were processed here. The ironworks did not last long though and were demolished in 1889, although some quarrying continued until the 1940s.

This is an alternative start/finish point for the walk.

Cross the stile at the bottom field corner beside Seend Wharf Bridge. ◀ Turn left along the road towards Seend Cleeve for 10 metres; across the road is the canalside Barge Inn. Turn left along the tarmac driveway towards Ferrum House and Dormer Cottage.

Keep right at two junctions (to the left is a view of Ferrum House with its turreted towers, built as the ironmaster's house – see Seend Ironworks later) to reach Pelch Lane in **Seend Cleeve** and bear right to a junction (150 metres down to the right is the Brewery Inn). Bear left gently uphill for 150 metres and turn right down Park

Lane, which soon becomes a track. At the split, keep left through a gate and follow the hedge-lined bridleway gently downhill for 500 metres.

Go through a gate, head across the field to the far right corner and cross Semington Brook. Keep ahead (aiming slightly left for a gate), following the bridleway through the next field; go through a gateway and fork right (footpath), staying close to the river. Cross two stiles at the corner and keep ahead through the next field to leave over a stile in the hedge opposite (right-hand corner).

Turn right along the lane for 50 metres, then turn right along the private road (bridleway) leading to Seend Park Farm. Keep right in front of the farmhouse and then pass to the right of a barn before crossing the swing bridge (156) over the canal.

> **Seend Park Farm** has an intriguing collection of memorabilia, while the adjacent oak timber-framed barn was constructed in 2000 and is based on a traditional Wiltshire barn.

Turn right and follow the towpath eastwards for 3.3km, passing five locks and five bridges (including bridge 153, with the Barge Inn on the opposite bank). At the sixth bridge (swing bridge 150), turn right across the canal to a path junction. Take the left-hand path across the field, go through a gate and keep ahead up through two fields, following the right-hand edge. Go through a gate in the top right corner and keep ahead along an enclosed track. Cross over the lane (Crooks Close to the left) and follow the path opposite – this soon becomes a track (driveway) – to reach the A361 at **Seend**.

Turn right; after 100 metres, once adjacent with Seend Lodge (right), turn left across the road to an area of grass with a circular tree seat. Keep ahead through a gate and follow the wide path between the wall (left) and hedge for 125 metres to a four-way junction. Turn right and follow the enclosed path, go through a gate and keep ahead across the field to the far side. Go through a gate

The colourful stained-glass Millennium Window in the Church of the Holy Cross, Seend

and bear right, following the path through the church-yard, keeping the **Holy Cross Church** over to your left. Exit through the gate and follow the walled driveway to the **A361** (75 metres to the left is the shop, 275 metres further on is the Bell Inn).

The village of **Seend**, which lies along the top of a ridge of greensand, was once part of the Royal Forest of Melksham. During the 15th and 16th centuries, many Wiltshire villages benefited from the wool industry, and the Holy Cross Church was rebuilt and enlarged during this time, partly funded by the wealthy clothier John Stokes (d.1498). Inside is the colourful stained-glass Millennium Window, depicting scenes from the area including the former ironworks. Along the main street there are a number of fine 17th- and 18th-century houses.

Cross over the road and turn right for 40 metres and then left along Rusty Lane back to the start.

WALK 16

Bradford-on-Avon, Avoncliff and Lower Westwood

Start/finish	Bradford-on-Avon Lock (14) and Wharf (ST 825 602); parking (pay-and-display) at Bradford Wharf (ST 826 601) – from B3109, head east along Moulton Drive, cross canal then left along Baileys Barn to its end
Distance	7.6km (4¾ miles)
Total ascent	125m
Time	2¼hr
Map	OS Explorer 156
Refreshments	Bradford-on-Avon: lots of choice; Avoncliff: the Cross Guns (01225 862335), No. 10 Tea Gardens (07725 853361); Lower Westwood: the New Inn (01225 863123)
Public transport	Trains to Bradford-on-Avon and Avoncliff; daily bus services to Bradford-on-Avon from Bath

From the wharf, the walk heads through bustling Bradford-on-Avon, crossing the River Avon via the medieval Town Bridge before passing a beautiful Saxon church. After crossing back over the River Avon, the route passes the stunning medieval Tithe Barn and then bears right along the canal to the impressive aqueduct at Avoncliff. Here the route leaves the canal, climbing up to Westwood, home to the 15th-century Westwood Manor (National Trust), before returning back to the start.

From the north end of the car park, exit onto the canal towpath and bear right (north) to Bradford-on-Avon Lock (14) and Wharf, passing the Kennet and Avon Canal Trust tea room; across the canal is the Barge Inn. Cross over the **B3109** (Frome Road) and turn right along the pavement, passing the Lock Inn Café and the Canal Tavern (both on the left). Keep ahead at the mini-roundabout, cross the railway and keep ahead at the next mini-roundabout; to the left is the railway station and car park (alternative start, ST 825 606).

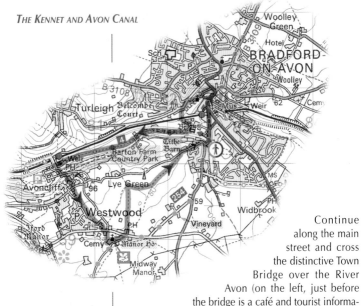

Continue along the main street and cross the distinctive Town Bridge over the River Avon (on the left, just before the bridge is a café and tourist information centre). Keep ahead to the junction (mini-roundabout) and bear right (straight on, B3107 signposted for Melksham) for 30 metres, then turn left across the road and left again along The Shambles. At its end, cross over the A363 and continue along Church Street, ignoring all side roads (shortly, on the left, is the former Abbey Mill, Bradford-on-Avon's last cloth mill, built in 1875). Keep to Church Street, past the Holy Trinity Church; on the right is the much smaller Saxon church.

The former wool town of **Bradford-on-Avon** – formed where the Saxons drove their carts across the 'broad ford', giving the early settlement its name – has a number of interesting buildings. The picturesque Town Bridge over the River Avon dates from the 13th century, although its distinctive dome-roofed lock-up was added during rebuilding in the 17th century; spot the brass gudgeon (fish) weathervane, which gives rise to the local saying 'under the fish and over the water'. Some of the buildings in The Shambles date from Tudor times, while along Church Street, opposite the much larger Holy Trinity Church, is St Laurence's Church, a wonderful example of Saxon architecture. To learn more about the town, visit the small local museum along Bridge Street.

Follow Church Street to its end and continue up the enclosed Church Lane (path) to a junction. Turn left along the lane, which soon swings left, heading downhill; with care, go through gates on either side of the railway. Keep ahead along the footpath through Barton Farm Country Park to cross the 14th-century four-arched stone packhorse bridge. Turn right for 20 metres and then fork left up beside the **Tithe Barn** (left), then go up the steps to join the canal towpath.

The magnificent 14th-century **Tithe Barn** (a 'tithe' was a tenth of a tenant's produce) used to be owned by Shaftesbury Abbey and is said to be one of the finest examples of a medieval monastic barn in the country.

The medieval Town Bridge across the River Avon at Bradford-on-Avon

The impressive aqueduct, which takes the canal across the River Avon, was built by John Rennie.

Turn right along the canal for 2km to reach **Avoncliff** (on the way passing the Boat Café), where the canal swings right and heads across the aqueduct. ◄ Do not cross the aqueduct, but turn sharp right towards the Cross Guns pub, which has a picturesque riverside terrace, and then turn sharp left under the aqueduct. Fork left up the steps and bear left along the lane, with the No. 10 Tea Gardens on the right and the canal over to the left.

Follow the lane as it curves left and then right, heading uphill; where it curves left again, go straight on across a private track, then pass through a gate and follow the path steeply up through the trees. Keep left at the split and continue up the narrow path to a minor road at **Westwood** (this consists of the hamlets of Lower and Upper Westwood). Go straight on to a junction. Turn left for a few metres and then right along a narrow path between the house (left) and car park (right). Follow the left-hand boundary and then keep ahead between the hedge and fence, with houses beyond.

The route passes 15th-century Westwood Manor, owned by the National Trust

Go straight on along the estate road for 40 metres and turn left through a gate into the field. Turn right and

follow the right-hand edge; ahead in the distance is the Westbury White Horse (Wiltshire's oldest white horse carving, first mentioned in 1742, although the current figure was cut in 1778). Ignore a path to the right and leave through a gate at the corner. Follow the enclosed path to an estate road and turn right. Turn left along the minor road and at the junction (left), turn right across the road and go through a gate to follow the enclosed path to a path junction. Turn left and follow the path past St Mary's Church to reach a minor road; on the left is the entrance to **Westwood Manor**.

> The small but interesting **Westwood Manor** dates from the 15th century with later additions and some lovely 17th-century plasterwork. The previous owner, Edgar Lister, was responsible for restoring the house to its former grandeur, including the panelling in the King's Room, brought from Keevil Manor in 1910; the manor is now owned by the National Trust (01225 863374).
>
> Parts of the adjacent **St Mary's Church** date from the late 12th-century, although much of the building was later rebuilt; inside there is some vivid 15th-century stained glass.

Bear left (straight on) along the lane to a junction and cross straight over, following the entrance drive beside the New Inn pub (right). At the end, enter the field and take the left-hand path straight on (north) through two fields to the far left corner. Once in the third field, turn right along the right-hand edge and continue through another field. In the next field, continue slightly left (mast on left) and then follow the left-hand boundary through three fields. Cross a stile and continue slightly left through the long field to leave over a stile beside a gate on the left, near the far-left corner. Bear right down the lane to the B3109. Cross over, turn left across the canal and then turn right, retracing the outward route back past the lock (14) to the car park on the left.

WALK 17

Avoncliff, Freshford, Monkton Combe and Dundas

Start/finish	Avoncliff railway station on north side of river (ST 804 600)
Distance	10.8km (6¾ miles)
Total ascent	230m
Time	3¼hr
Map	OS Explorer 142, 155 and 156
Refreshments	Avoncliff: the Cross Guns (01225 862335), No. 10 Tea Gardens (07725 853361); Freshford: the Inn (01225 722250), the Galleries shop and café (01225 723249); Monkton Combe: the Wheelwrights Arms (01225 722287); Brassknocker Basin: the Angelfish Café (01225 723483)
Public transport	Trains to Avoncliff and Freshford; bus services between Trowbridge and Bath stop at Freshford, Monkton Combe and Dundas (excluding Sundays)
Note	The walk may also be started from Avoncliff car park (ST 804 599) on south side of river, west of Bradford-on-Avon.

From the impressive Avoncliff Aqueduct, the walk heads alongside the River Avon to call in at Freshford, before crossing the A36 and passing Limpley Stoke where Bath stone is still mined. The route then makes a steep descent to Monkton Combe before passing under the A36 to visit the Somerset Coal Canal at Brassknocker Basin. The last leg of the walk follows the canal as it sweeps along the valley from Dundas Aqueduct back to Avoncliff.

From the railway station at Avoncliff, head up the steps and turn left across the aqueduct and then immediately turn sharp left down towards the Cross Guns (a 17th-century pub with riverside terrace), then left again to follow the tarmac track under the aqueduct. Keep ahead along the track, with buildings on the left. If starting from the

Avoncliff car park, exit the car park and turn left along the track, keeping buildings on the left, as it swings left away from the aqueduct.

> The picturesque hamlet of **Avoncliff**, tucked in the valley beside the River Avon, is home to the Avoncliff Aqueduct, built by John Rennie to carry the canal across the river. Water from the river was used to power mills here, dating from the 16th century.

Follow the track past Ancliff Square (left) and at the end of the track keep ahead through a gate. ▸ Follow the path through another gate and continue through the field with the River Avon on the right. At the far side, go through a gate and keep ahead with Avoncliff Wood on the left. Go through a gate to enter a field, where the path splits; take the right-hand fork heading west across the field and leave through a gate beside the 16th-century

Ancliff Square was built in the late 18th century as a group of weavers' cottages and was later used as a workhouse.

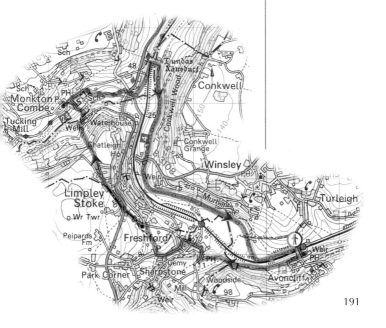

191

bridge at **Freshford**. Turn right over the bridge, crossing the River Frome, and follow the lane past the Inn at Freshford. Keep to the road as it swings left and rises; Station Road on the right leads to Freshford railway station (300 metres each way).

At the top of the rise, where the main street swings left, keep ahead to reach St Peter's Church on the right; from the churchyard there is a great view of the village. Keep ahead down the lane and follow it to the left and then left again to a crossroads, with a school opposite.

The village of **Freshford** dates back to Saxon times and a mill was mentioned in the Domesday Book, although Roman remains found in the area point to a much older settlement. Parts of St Peter's Church date back to the 14th and 15th centuries.

Go straight across, following the lane for 350 metres. Turn right along the track between the Galleries shop and café (right) and village hall (left). Keep ahead past the play area and then go up through the field, aiming slightly right. Leave through a gate at the top and pass St Mary's Church to join a lane in **Limpley Stoke**; parts of St Mary's Church date from the 10th century, with later additions and alterations.

Turn left along the lane for 350 metres to the A36 (Warminster Road). With care, cross straight over and follow Midford Lane opposite for 550 metres, soon passing the entrance to the Stoke Hill Mine; this extensive underground quarry still produces large quantities of Bath stone. At the Y-junction, fork right along the lane – Old Track – for 150 metres; where this swings right, go straight on, soon heading steeply down a sunken bridleway to a track.

To visit the Victorian St Michael's Church, turn left along the lane for 75 metres; from the church, retrace the route back to the junction with Mill Lane and keep ahead.

Turn right for a few metres and then left down the narrow bridleway. Keep ahead across two footbridges crossing the Midford Brook and then up Mill Lane in **Monkton Combe**, passing the dome-roofed former 18th-century lock-up. At the T-junction, beside the Wheelwright Arms pub (left), the walk turns right. ◄

The view of Freshford from St Peter's Church

Follow the lane (Church Lane) north-eastwards; once past the school, which dominates a large part of the village, turn right beside the buildings (signposted as National Cycle Route 24 to Bath and Chippenham). Keep left to follow the path as it skirts left round the lower edge of the sports hall and then go down steps to a lane. Turn left along the lane (cycle route) for 500 metres, passing under the A36, then turn left at the entrance to the Somerset Coal Canal Visitor Centre.

The **Somerset Coal Canal**, which opened in 1805, was built by the owners of several North Somerset coal mines to transport coal to Bath and Bristol. The canal was initially successful, carrying over 100,000 tons of coal a year in the 1820s. However, competition from the railway led to its closure in 1898. The first 500 metres from its junction with the Kennet and Avon Canal have been restored, although the Somersetshire Coal Canal Society has plans to restore more of the canal (www.coalcanal.org).

Go through the gate and turn right. Where the route splits, fork left up the gravel track (permissive route) to reach the Angelfish Café on the left beside the Somerset Coal Canal; the right-hand fork leads to a car park and then continues to Dundas Aqueduct. ▶ Bear right and follow the canalside path for 250 metres before continuing along the tarmac track to reach the Kennet and Avon

If the gate is locked, follow the B3108 to the A36, turn right along the pavement for 400 metres and fork right down the track to Dundas Wharf and the aqueduct.

193

The impressive Dundas Aqueduct

Canal beside the **Dundas Aqueduct**; Dundas Wharf and the junction with the Somerset Coal Canal are just to the left.

Like the aqueduct at Avoncliff, the **Dundas Aqueduct** was built by John Rennie to take the canal over the River Avon; at the eastern end, steps down to the right give a better view of the impressive structure.

Turn right across the aqueduct (viewing steps on right) and follow the canal for 4.2km, passing two bridges; the first bridge (175) carries the **B3108** across the canal. At **Avoncliff**, follow the canal as it swings right to cross the aqueduct; ahead on the right is the car park. For the railway station, immediately after crossing the aqueduct turn right and right again down steps to pass under the aqueduct, heading towards the Cross Guns pub and then turn sharp right back up to the canal. Turn right back across the east side of the aqueduct to access the station on the right.

WALK 18

Dundas Aqueduct, Monkton Farleigh and Bathford

Start/finish	Lay-by (with bus stop) on east side of the A36 at Dundas Aqueduct (ST 783 625), 350 metres north of the Monkton Combe junction
Distance	13.7km (8½ miles)
Total ascent	270m
Time	4hr
Map	OS Explorer 155 and 156
Refreshments	Monkton Farleigh: the Muddy Duck (01225 858705); Bathford: the Crown (01225 852426); Bathampton: the Raft Café Boat, the George Inn (01225 425079)
Public transport	Bus services to Dundas (A36) from Bath and Trowbridge (excluding Sundays)

A great day walk with some steep ascents and descents, taking in lovely views across the Avon Valley and a sweeping section of the canal. After crossing the impressive Dundas Aqueduct, the route meanders through fields following the River Avon before rising to pass through Pinckney Green and arrive at Monkton Farleigh, whose village pub – the Muddy Duck – is reputedly Wiltshire's most haunted. The walk then heads to Bathford Hill to visit Brown's Folly, where you can admire the views before heading down to Bathford and then continuing towards Bathampton. The final leg follows the canal back to the start, passing the historic Claverton Pumping Station on the way.

From the north (Bath) end of the lay-by on the east side of the A36, turn right down a signposted path to Dundas Wharf; the former Somerset Coal Canal joined here from the small bridge on the right. Turn left (signposted to Claverton) with the Kennet and Avon Canal on the right, then turn right over the footbridge (177) and turn right again following the left side of the canal as it swings left to cross **Dundas Aqueduct**.

Dundas Wharf, with its old cast-iron crane, is home to the impressive **Dundas Aqueduct**, built by John Rennie to take the canal over the River Avon; it also marks the junction with the Somerset Coal Canal. The canal, which opened in 1805, was built by the owners of several North Somerset coal mines to allow the easy transportation of coal to Bath and Bristol. Despite its initial success, competition from the railway lead to its closure in 1898. The first 500 metres to Brassknocker Basin, home to the Angelfish Café (01225 723483), have been restored.

Immediately after crossing the aqueduct and before the canal swings right, turn left down steps through the trees. Continue through the field with trees on the right and then keep ahead to the far left field corner, beside the River Avon. Cross a stile and continue, following the river for 1km, crossing a couple of footbridges. After passing another stile and footbridge, the path heads diagonally right away from the river, passing some bushes and trees. Go through a gate and turn right up beside the fence and then through another gate. Follow the enclosed path ahead; from here, admire the views of Claverton to the west across the valley.

Keep ahead through Sheephouse Farm and turn left along the lane for 250 metres. At the house on the left, turn right through a gate in the hedge and follow the tree-shaded path uphill, passing another gate. Keep ahead alongside the stone wall, cross a stone stile and continue straight on through the archway under the A363.

Keep ahead past a cottage and follow the enclosed route as it swings right to a minor road. Cross straight over and follow the lane through **Pinckney Green**, keeping left at the junction and soon rejoining the minor

The Muddy Duck pub at Monkton Farleigh is said to be Wiltshire's most haunted

road. Keep ahead (northwards) along the pavement for 675 metres towards **Monkton Farleigh**. Some 50 metres after Broadstones (road on right), turn right along a driveway (footpath sign) for 100 metres and at the slight left bend go straight on over a stile. Pass through gates and follow a path through the churchyard, keeping left of St Peter's Church.

Turn left up the road and at the second junction, with the Muddy Duck pub ahead and left, fork right along the road signposted for Kingsdown. Where the lane swings right, turn left along the track. Cross a stile and keep ahead along the enclosed route; ahead and left is the Monk's Conduit (private).

> **Monkton Farleigh** was once home to a Cluniac priory founded in the early 12th century, but all that remains visible now is a small stone building known as the Monk's Conduit, which sheltered the spring that supplied water to the priory; the manor house (not visible) stands on the site of the former priory. Parts of St Peter's Church date from the 12th century, although most of it was rebuilt in the 19th century. The village pub, the unusually named Muddy Duck, is reputed to be Wiltshire's most haunted. A quick look at the OS 1:25,000 map will reveal a number of 'air shafts' – these are remnants from the underground mines where Bath stone was once quarried; the tunnels were used during World War II as a large ammunition storage facility.

Cross straight over a minor road and take the track opposite. Go through a gate and follow the left-hand field margin. Cross a lane and pass just right of a small building, heading through trees to a track. Dogleg left and continue in the same direction on the grassy strip between fields towards the trees on **Bathford Hill**. Keep ahead between stone walls to a path junction and turn right, following the wall on the right to reach **Brown's Folly**. Turn left through a gate.

Brown's Folly, high above the River Avon on Bathford Hill – from here there are spectacular views of Bath

Brown's Folly was built in 1845 by Wade Browne, a local quarry owner. The nature reserve (managed by the Avon Wildlife Trust) has a number of outcrops where Bath stone (oolitic limestone – see 'Geology' section in the Introduction) was mined. These disused mines now provide roosting sites for bats, including the greater horseshoe bat, one of the rarest mammals in the UK (13 of the 18 UK bat species can be found at the reserve). Plants include several types of orchid and the nationally scarce Bath asparagus (or spiked star of Bethlehem), a tall plant that flowers with green and white flowers in June/July.

Head steeply downhill (steps, with old quarry workings to the right) for 50 metres to a path junction and turn left through a gate. Follow the level path for 150 metres before turning sharp right down through the trees. Cross diagonally right over the track and continue down through the trees. Exit the woods and head north-west diagonally down across the field to the bottom right corner.

Cross a stile and turn left down the grassy path, then down the estate road (Mountain Wood) to a T-junction in **Bathford**. Turn right past Manor Farm Cottage and then left down the enclosed footpath between buildings, later passing to the right of St Swithun's Church.

> **Bathford**, originally known as Forde, has a history stretching back to Roman times. A Roman road crossed the By Brook hereabouts, to join with the Fosse Way that led through Bath; the bridge over the By Brook was built in the 13th or 14th century to replace the ford. Parts of St Swithun's Church date from the 12th century and the churchyard is the resting place of Admiral Horatio Nelson's sister, Ann.

Cross over Church Street and follow Ostling Lane, which soon swings right and heads steeply downhill to a junction beside the Crown pub (right). Cross over the road (Bathford Hill) and turn left (north-west) to follow the pavement alongside the A363. Cross the By Brook via the footbridge beside the medieval road bridge; just before the railway bridge (built by Isambard Kingdom Brunel), turn left across the road (A363).

Take the signed footpath opposite as it rises up beside the railway to cross the River Avon and then drops down to a gate. Bear diagonally right (south-west) across the field, passing a large pylon, to the far side; with care, go through gates either side of the **railway**. Go straight on along the lane for 300 metres and turn left after the last house to join the canal towpath; to the right (west) along the towpath is the Raft Café Boat and just beyond the bridge is the George Inn and St Nicholas' Church in **Bathampton**. ◄

St Nicholas' Church, dating from the 13th century, houses a memorial to Admiral Arthur Phillip, the first Governor of New South Wales, Australia.

The route turns left (east) and follows the canal towpath for 4.8km back to Dundas Wharf. After 3km, at bridge 179, a 150-metre detour down Ferry Lane to the left leads to **Claverton Pumping Station**, just across the railway.

A short detour leads to the historic Claverton Pumping Station

To supply water to this section of the canal, John Rennie built **Claverton Pumping Station** in 1813. The pump, which was used to lift water 14.5m up to the canal, is powered by a waterwheel driven by the River Avon. The pump operated for close to 140 years before falling derelict with the gradual decline of the canal. Fortunately, dedicated volunteers have brought this remarkable piece of engineering back to full working order, although these days electric pumps are used to provide water to the canal. (Opening times: 01225 483001.)

Looking back along the footpath to the footbridge (177) at Dundas Wharf

The route continues alongside the canal, passing a swing bridge. At the footbridge (177), turn right across the canal and bear left alongside Dundas Wharf, before turning right and following the path back up to the lay-by on the A36.

WALK 19
Bathampton, Sham Castle and Bath

Start/finish	St Nicholas' Church, Bathampton (ST 776 665), off the A36; car park opposite church
Alternative start/finish	Bath Spa railway station (ST 752 643)
Distance	11.9km (7½ miles); alternative start/finish: add 0.4km (¼ mile)
Total ascent	230m; alternative start/finish: add 0m
Time	3½hr; alternative start/finish: add 0hr
Map	OS Explorer 155
Refreshments	Bathampton: the George Inn (01225 425079), the Raft Café Boat; Bath: lots of choice
Public transport	Trains to Bath; bus services to Bathampton and Bath
Note	The walk can be shortened by missing out the loop through the centre of Bath. This reduces the walk length by 3.1km (2 miles), the ascent by 40m, and the time by 1hr.

From Bathampton, the walk follows the canal for a while before heading up Bathampton Down to visit Sham Castle. After admiring the great view of Bath, the route heads down towards Bath and follows the canal past several locks to reach Widcombe Lock, where the man-made canal joins the River Avon. From here, the route meanders past some of Bath's most impressive sights, including Pulteney Bridge, the Abbey, the Royal Crescent – Bath's Georgian masterpiece and grandest architectural statement – and The Circus, before heading through Sydney Gardens and following the canal back to Bathampton.

Alternative start from Bath Spa railway station
Exit from Platform 1 (south side of station), cross the footbridge and turn left alongside the road (A36) for 100 metres. Then turn left along the lane to a bridge over the canal, beside Widcombe Lock (7), to join up with the main route at a point shown by a margin note below.

Inside St Nicholas' Church, dating from the 13th century, is the Australia Chapel and the grave of Admiral Arthur Phillip, the first Governor of New South Wales, Australia.

From St Nicholas' Church in Bathampton, turn left (south) past the George Inn to reach the canal, then turn right; just to the left, beyond the bridge (183), is the Raft Café Boat. ◄

Follow the canal south-westwards for 800 metres, passing a picturesque row of cottages (right); in 1897, art teacher William Harbutt invented plasticine and in 1900 opened a plasticine factory (now demolished) on the opposite side of the canal. Pass under Candy's Bridge (184) and immediately turn right to cross a stone stile, then turn right and right again to cross the canal. Follow Meadow Lane uphill and turn right along Bathampton Lane to the **A36**. With care, cross straight over and follow the track uphill. Pass a gate and keep left (straight on) up through the trees on **Bathampton Down** for 350 metres. Pass another gate and fork right, then right again at a marker post and follow the level path through the long field (golf course on left, trees on right). Pass to the right of the radio mast and follow the track ahead for 500 metres.

This 18th-century folly was commissioned by Ralph Allen to improve the view from his home in Bath.

Keep straight on past the clubhouse to reach **Sham Castle**. ◄ Stand with your back to the castle and admire the great view of Bath before heading west, down a path through the trees, slightly to the right, then cross straight over the access road for the golf course (or head back to

Sham Castle on Bathampton Down offers a great view of Bath

Cleveland House straddles the canal

the clubhouse and turn left). Go through a gate and follow the path steeply down through the field before leaving through another gate. Cross over North Lane and turn right for 100 metres, then go left down the enclosed path.

Cross straight over Cleveland Walk (road) and head down Sham Castle Lane in **Bathwick**. Turn right at the bottom and keep left to reach Sydney Road. Turn sharp left, doubling back along the path, to join the canal beside Cleveland House, which stands over a short tunnel. Originally built by the Duke of Cleveland, the house

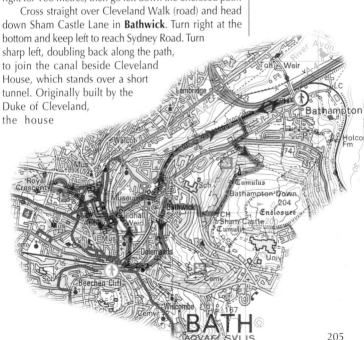

205

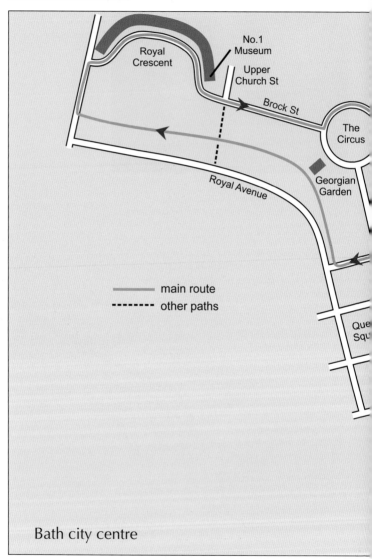

Bath city centre

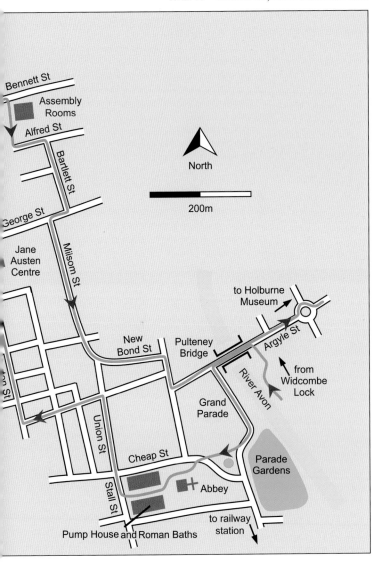

North

200m

Bennett St

Assembly Rooms

Alfred St

Bartlett St

George St

Jane Austen Centre

Milsom St

to Holburne Museum

New Bond St

Pulteney Bridge

Argyle St

River Avon

from Widcombe Lock

Union St

Grand Parade

Cheap St

Parade Gardens

Stall St

Abbey

Pump House and Roman Baths

to railway station

was the head office of the Kennet & Avon Canal Company between 1825 and 1864.

Follow the canal southwards (canal on right) and at the next bridge (188) cross over to the right-hand side via the bridge. Continue along the canal (with the canal on your left), passing Bath Top Lock (13); along the way, on the left, is the former Baird's Maltings building, where grain was soaked in water, then sprouted and dried to produce malt for beer.

Continue past two more locks (beside lock 11 is the Pump Shed refreshments kiosk and an ornate chimney from the former steam pump house – see Thimble Mill below). Cross over the minor road and continue past another lock (10) to reach Bath Deep Lock (8/9); this lock was formed when the road was built over the canal by combining locks 8 and 9 to form the deepest lock along the canal and second deepest in England, with a rise and fall of 5.7m.

CITY OF BATH

The City of Bath, a World Heritage Site, offers an extensive list of interesting sights. Its history stretches back to at least the Iron Age, when the hot springs here were dedicated to the goddess Sul. It was the Romans who established Bath as a bathing mecca, renaming the town Aquae Sulis, or 'water of Sulis'. The importance of the baths declined after the demise of the Roman empire in Britain, until eventually a new bathing complex was built in the 16th century. Subsequent renovations by the Victorians unearthed the original Roman Baths that can be seen today.

The development of the Georgian spa town is mostly attributed to Richard 'Beau' Nash, a celebrated dandy and leader of fashion in 18th-century Britain; to Ralph Allen, onetime postmaster and owner of several Bath stone quarries; and to the architects John Wood the Elder, his son John Wood the Younger, and Robert Adam.

The magnificent Bath Abbey was built on the site of an earlier Norman abbey, which itself replaced an earlier Anglo-Saxon church where the first King of England, King Edgar, was crowned in AD973. The current building dates from the early 16th century and has been described as the last great Gothic church in England.

At the main road, turn left across the canal and immediately turn left and then left again down some steps to pass under the road. Follow the canal under another bridge to reach Widcombe Lock (7), where the canal joins the Avon Navigation and the River Avon; turn right across the bridge (194). ▶ Beside the canal is the former Thimble Mill, originally built to house a steam-driven pump that raised water from the river up to lock 11, where there was another pump to raise water up to lock 13.

Keep ahead with the River Avon on the left, pass under the railway bridge, follow Spring Gardens Road for a short way and then keep left, still following the river, and pass under a road bridge. Keep beside the river, go up the steps and turn left across the shop-lined **Pulteney Bridge**, designed by Robert Adams in 1773. ▶

At the junction, turn left along **Grand Parade** (A3039) for 100 metres; from the left-hand (east) side of Grand Parade there is a great view of Pulteney Bridge and the weir. As the road curves right (with **Parade Gardens** ahead), turn right to cross Grand Parade and head past the former Empire Hotel (right); on the left is a small circular garden with an obelisk erected in 1734 to commemorate

The alternative route from Bath Spa railway station joins the walk here.

For the shorter walk, turn right along Argyle Street and then continue along Great Pulteney Street, following the last part of the main walk.

The elegant Pulteney Bridge and weir – just one of the many impressive sights that Bath has to offer

the Prince of Orange's visit to Bath to take the waters. Cross over a road and continue along the right-hand side of **Bath Abbey**, then dogleg left to continue through the Abbey Churchyard (paved square) with the **Pump House** and **Roman Baths** on the left.

Leave through the columned arcade and turn right along **Stall Street**. Cross over Cheap Street and follow the pedestrianised Union Street straight on to a junction. Turn left along Upper Borough Walls to its end and turn right along Barton Street. Ignore side roads and keep ahead past the tree-lined **Queen Square**. Keep ahead at the crossroads up Gay Street for 50 metres, passing the **Jane Austen Centre** (01225 443000) at number 40. ◄ Turn left along Queen Parade Place for 50 metres and turn right up the steps just before **Royal Avenue**, following a path signposted for the Royal Crescent; as it curves left, on the right is the **Georgian Garden** (open most days).

At the cross-path junction, keep ahead alongside the trees to a road. Turn right uphill and then right again following the cobbled street past the impressive **Royal Crescent**. At the far side, pass the museum (**No. 1 Royal Crescent**) and keep ahead along Brock Street to **The Circus**.

The world-famous romantic novelist visited Bath on a number of occasions and set much of Northanger Abbey and Persuasion here.

> The beautiful curving **Royal Crescent**, built in the Palladian style and dating from 1766, is the masterpiece of the architect John Wood the Younger; Number 1 Royal Crescent is now a museum decorated and furnished as it might have been during the period 1776–96 (01225 428126). The elegant **Circus** was designed by John Wood the Elder in 1754; the portrait and landscape painter Thomas Gainsborough lived at number 17 between 1760 and 1774.

Circle clockwise and take the first exit left (Bennett Street) for 50 metres. Turn right on a path past the **Assembly Rooms** (left), then left along Alfred Street for 50 metres. ◄ Turn right down Bartlett Street, cross over at the traffic lights and turn right, then left down Milsom Street, later curving left along New Bond Street. At the junction,

The Assembly Rooms (01225 477173), along with the Pump Rooms, were at the centre of Bath's social scene in the 18th and 19th centuries.

turn right along Northgate Street then left along Bridge Street to recross **Pulteney Bridge**.

Follow Argyle Street and then Great Pulteney Street (Bath's grand boulevard lined with matching Georgian houses, designed by Thomas Baldwin for Sir William Pulteney) to a junction with the **Holburne Museum** opposite. Cross over and follow Sydney Place with the museum on the left before turning left through a gateway to enter Sydney Gardens.

> The **Holburne Museum** (01225 388569) is home to an impressive collection of art, silverware and porcelain, much of it collected by Sir William Holburne. This grand Georgian mansion, with its columns and pediments, has been a museum since 1916, but was originally built as a ballroom and coffee house overlooking the Sydney Pleasure Gardens.

Follow the tarmac path, keeping left at the first junction, and then turn right along a wide tarmac path. Cross the bridge over the railway beside the columned temple and keep ahead. Just before the bridge over the canal, turn right then left through a gate to join the towpath. Turn left alongside the canal, passing under the wrought-iron bridge and then through a short tunnel. Follow the canal for 2.2km, passing a footbridge then Candy's Bridge (184), passed earlier in the walk, to reach **Bathampton**. After passing the George Inn, turn left back to the church.

WALK 20

*Saltford, Swineford, North Stoke
and the Cotswold Way*

Start/finish	Newbridge Park and Ride (ST 717 657) on the A4, just on the western edge of Bath; roadside parking on the south side of the A4 opposite Newbridge Park and Ride entrance
Distance	15km (9¼ miles)
Total ascent	285m
Time	4½hr
Map	OS Explorer 155
Refreshments	Newbridge: the Boathouse (01225 482584); Saltford: the Riverside Inn (01225 873862), the Bird in Hand (01225 873335); Swineford: the Swan (0117 932 3101)
Public transport	Daily bus service to Newbridge (A4) from Bath

From Newbridge Road (A4), the route follows the River Avon Trail downstream to Saltford, home to an old brass mill, before joining a short section of the Bristol & Bath Railway Path as far as Avon Riverside Station. The walk then heads upstream for a short way to arrive at Swineford. From here, it's a stiff climb up through picturesque North Stoke to the earthworks of an Iron Age hill fort on Little Down. The return follows a section of the Cotswold Way, offering some great views as it heads back towards Bath.

From the entrance to Newbridge Park and Ride, turn right along the north side of the A4 (bus stop to left), cross the River Avon via New Bridge and immediately turn right down the path and bear right along the track. Keep to the right of the trees and follow the riverside path downstream along field edges, with the River Avon on the right. After 1.4km, pass under the old railway bridge and continue as the path and river swing right, soon with Isambard Kingdom Brunel's Great Western Railway line,

From Newbridge, the walk follows the River Avon downstream

which opened in 1841, on the left; the large house across the river is **Kelston Park**. ▶

Follow the path past Saltford Rowing Club, keeping close to the river. Cross a footbridge over the entrance to **Saltford Marina** and follow the track to the Riverside Inn, with a weir and Kelston Lock (5) on the right. As the tarmac track swings left, go straight on for a short way before turning left along the enclosed path away from the river to a road. Turn right along the road, soon passing Saltford Brass Mill.

> **Saltford Brass Mill**, now a scheduled ancient monument, is the only surviving copper and brass mill built along the Avon Valley. Although closed in 1925, the mill has been fully restored and is open at certain times (0117 986 2216).

Keep ahead past a parking and picnic area (left) to reach a T-junction beside the Bird in Hand pub. Turn right down the road; just before the old railway bridge, fork right up the steps and turn left. The route follows the old railway – now the Bristol & Bath Railway Path (part of National Cycle Route 4) – for 1.4km.

The mid-18th-century house was built by John Wood the Younger for Sir Caesar Hawkins, Serjeant-Surgeon to Kings George II and III; Capability Brown designed the adjoining parkland.

The **Bristol & Bath Railway Path** follows the course of the former branch line between Bath and Mangotsfield, which was opened by the Midland Railway Company in 1869; the line closed in the 1960s. A 5km section now forms the Avon Valley Railway between Avon Riverside Station and Oldland Station; the heritage railway operates steam-hauled services during the summer (0117 932 5538).

Continue past **Avon Riverside Station**; after crossing the bridge over the River Avon, fork left down the tarmac path, which swings left down to a picnic area and landing stage beside the river.

Turn left to go under the railway bridge and follow the riverside path (river on right) through fields to join the A431 opposite the Swan pub at **Swineford**. Cross over and turn left for 75 metres, then right along the lane signposted for the Swineford Picnic Area. After 150 metres, just after passing a house on the right and before the picnic area, turn right alongside the wall (the old watercourse on the left is all that remains of the former iron foundry). Go through a gate and keep ahead, following the path up across two fields. At the top edge, leave through a gate and follow the tree-shaded sunken route steeply uphill. At the top, where the track swings left, go straight on through a gate and follow the enclosed path, which soon swings left following a hedge, to reach a lane in **North Stoke**, at a bend.

The picturesque village of **North Stoke** has a history going back over 2000 years. Overlooking the village, on Little Down, are the earthworks of a former promontory Iron Age hill fort, while in the village, Church Farm is built on the site of a Roman villa; St Martin's Church is slightly more recent, dating from the 12th century.

Go straight on uphill to Church Farm (left); ahead up the steps is **St Martin's Church**. Follow the track to the left and right, then continue uphill for 700 metres to a path junction and marker post and turn sharp right; the walk now follows the **Cotswold Way** (CW) for 4.5km towards Bath. ▶ Head south-west along the level path (CW) for 450 metres, soon passing through a gate; from this lofty location on **Little Down** there are some great views to the west.

At the path junction, beside the fence corner (left), turn left. Leave the field and follow the grassy strip straight on. After passing through the eastern earthworks of the former Iron Age hill fort, turn right and then left at the field corner. Follow the right-hand

The Cotswold Way National Trail runs for 164km (102 miles) along the Cotswold escarpment from Chipping Camden to Bath.

The Swan pub at Swineford, below the Cotswold escarpment

field edge heading south-east for 500 metres (over to the left is Bath Racecourse on Lansdown Hill, which at 235m above sea level is England's highest racecourse) to reach **Prospect Stile** (now a gate) and adjacent toposcope; from here there is a wonderful view, including Westbury White Horse (south-east, 25km), Alfred's Tower (south, 33km) and Pen Hill Mast (south-west, 25km).

Go through the gate and follow the path (CW), which soon swings right and heads downhill for 350 metres, passing a gate to reach a staggered cross-junction. Turn left through a gate, then immediately right through another gate and continue along the enclosed bridleway (CW).

After 475 metres, a gate on the right gives permissive access up to **Kelston Round Hill**. Follow the path uphill and circle counter-clockwise round the fenced trees, admiring the changing views: west towards Wales, south-west to the Mendip Hills, south-east to Bath and east to the Wiltshire Downs, with Beckford's Tower nearby (built in 1827 by the author William Beckford). Cross a stile and after passing the trig point head south-eastwards down across the field; leave through a gate and continue along the Cotswold Way (adds 200 metres).

Follow the enclosed bridleway (CW) steeply down to Pendean Farm. Ignore the road down to the left and go straight on to enter a field. Follow the path as it contours round **Dean Hill**. Leave the field and continue steeply downhill, soon passing a **trig point** on Penn Hill. Keep straight on down through the field to reach the recreation ground and turn right along the right-hand edge.

Cross over Penn Hill Road and turn right, passing three side roads. As the road bears down to the left, cross over and go straight on along the lane and then along an enclosed route as it swings left and heads down past a school. At the main road (**A431**), cross via the traffic lights and turn right. Once level with the school entrance (right), turn left through a gate and follow the narrow path down through the trees. At the bottom, pass to the left of the rowing club buildings, cross straight over the track and follow the enclosed path (over to the right is the Boathouse pub). Keep ahead across the access drive (pub to right) and go up the steps to the A4. Turn left alongside the road for 150 metres back to the **Newbridge Park and Ride** entrance on the left.

APPENDIX A

Route summary tables

STAGE SUMMARY TABLE

Stage	Start	Grid ref	Finish	Grid ref	Distance – km (miles)	Cumulative – km (miles)	Ascent (m)	Time (hr)	Page
1	Reading	SU 730 738	Woolhampton	SU 572 665	20.7 (12¾)	20.7 (12¾)	100	5½	28
2	Woolhampton	SU 572 665	Hungerford	SU 338 687	24.9 (15½)	45.6 (28¼)	180	6½	36
3	Hungerford	SU 338 687	Pewsey Wharf	SU 157 610	22.8 (14¼)	68.4 (42½)	150	6	46
4	Pewsey Wharf	SU 157 610	Devizes	SU 005 618	19.3 (12)	87.7 (54½)	160	5	56
5	Devizes	SU 005 618	Bradford-on-Avon	ST 825 602	20.1 (12½)	107.8 (67)	100	5¼	64
6	Bradford-on-Avon	ST 825 602	Bath	ST 753 643	15.7 (9¾)	123.5 (76¾)	80	4	74
7	Bath	ST 753 643	Bristol	ST 585 728	28.6 (17¾)	152.1 (94½)	85	7¼	84

WALK SUMMARY TABLE

Walk	Start/finish	Start grid ref	Distance – km (miles)	Ascent (m)	Time (hr)	Page
1	Reading railway station	SU 714 738	6.8 (4¼)	45	2	100
2	Aldermaston railway station	SU 601 673	9.1 (5¾)	65	2½	107
3	Thatcham railway station	SU 527 663	12.7 (8) or 9.6 (6)	100 or 95	3½ or 2½	112

Walk	Start/finish	Start grid ref	Distance – km (miles)	Ascent (m)	Time (hr)	Page
4	Newbury Wharf or railway station	SU 473 672 or SU 472 667	7.6 (4¾) or 8.4 (5¼)	90	2 or 2¼	117
5	Kintbury railway station	SU 386 671	9.6 (6)	125	2¾	124
6	Hungerford	SU 340 685	11.6 (7¼)	105	3¼	129
7	Hungerford Town Hall or railway station	SU 337 685 or SU 340 685	11.2 (7) or 11.6 (7¼)	110	3	135
8	Great Bedwyn	SU 279 645	9.5 (6)	135	2½	142
9	Wootton Rivers	SU 198 629	12 (7½)	105	3¼	147
10	Pewsey Wharf or railway station	SU 157 610 or SU 160 604	10.5 (6½) or 12.1 (7½)	230 or 250	3 or 3½	154
11	Wilcot	SU 143 611	9.7 (6)	125	2¾	158
12	All Cannings Bridge or Alton Barnes	SU 076 622 or SU 115 638	12.1 (7½) or 13.2 (8¼)	255 or 285	3¾ or 4¼	162
13	All Cannings Bridge	SU 076 622	14.5 (9)	250	4¼	168
14	Devizes Wharf	SU 004 617	10.5 (6½)	110	3	174
15	Seend	ST 943 611	9.2 (5¾)	120	2½	180
16	Bradford-on-Avon	ST 825 602	7.6 (4¾)	125	2¼	185
17	Avoncliff	ST 804 600	10.8 (6¾)	230	3¼	190
18	Dundas	ST 783 625	13.7 (8½)	270	4	195
19	Bathampton or Bath Spa railway station	ST 776 665 or ST 752 643	11.9 (7½) or 12.3 (7¾)	230	3½	203
20	Newbridge (Bath)	ST 717 657	15 (9¼)	285	4½	212

APPENDIX B
Itinerary planner

Accommodation: 1 = campsite or hostel; 2 = B&B; 3 = pub with rooms, or hotel
Bus services may be limited and/or irregular, and may not operate on Sundays
Bold rows indicate places where it would be easy to split the stages on the long-distance route

Place	Intermediate distance – km (miles)	Cumulative – km (miles)	Shop	Pub/café	Accomm	Bus	Train
Reading	0 (0)	0 (0)	✓		2, 3	✓	✓
Burghfield Bridge	7.3 (4½)	7.3 (4½)		✓		✓	
Theale	**3.9 (2½)**	**11.2 (7)**	✓	✓	3	✓	✓
Tyle Mill	2.5 (1½)	13.7 (8½)		✓		✓	
Sulhamstead: 0.8km (½ mile) off route	0 (0)	13.7 (8½)			2		
Ufton Bridge	1.1 (¾)	14.8 (9¼)					
Aldermaston Wharf	2.5 (1½)	17.3 (10¾)		✓	3	✓	✓
Aldermaston: 2.3km (1½ miles) off route	0 (0)	17.3 (10¾)		✓	3	✓	
Woolhampton	**3.4 (2)**	**20.7 (12¾)**	✓	✓		✓	✓
Midgham: 0.5km (¼ mile) off route	2.3 (1½)	23.0 (14¼)	✓	✓	2, 3	✓	
Thatcham	2.4 (1½)	25.4 (15¾)	✓	✓	2, 3	✓	✓
Newbury	**5.9 (3¾)**	**31.3 (19½)**	✓	✓	1, 2, 3	✓	✓

Place	Intermediate distance – km (miles)	Cumulative – km (miles)	Shop	Pub/café	Accomm	Bus	Train
Marsh Benham	5.3 (3¼)	36.6 (22¾)		✓			
Kintbury	3.8 (2¼)	40.4 (25)	✓	✓	3	✓	✓
Hungerford	**5.2 (3¼)**	**45.6 (28¼)**	✓	✓	**2, 3**	✓	✓
Froxfield: 0.35km (¼ mile) off route	3.6 (2¼)	49.2 (30½)		✓	3	✓	
Great Bedwyn	**4.3 (2¾)**	**53.5 (33¼)**	✓	✓		✓	✓
Crofton	2.9 (1¾)	56.4 (35)		✓	2		
Wilton: 1km (¾ mile) off route	0 (0)	56.4 (35)		✓			
Wolfhall: 1.1km (¾ mile) off route	2 (1¼)	58.4 (36¼)			1, 2		
Stibb Green: 1km (¾ mile) off route	1.3 (¾)	59.7 (37)		✓		✓	
Burbage: 2km (1½ miles) off route	0 (0)	59.7 (37)		✓		✓	
Wootton Rivers	3.9 (2½)	63.6 (39½)	✓	✓	2, 3		
Easton Royal: 1.9km (1¼ miles) off route	0 (0)	63.6 (39½)		✓	1, 2		
Pewsey Wharf	**4.8 (3)**	**68.4 (42½)**		✓		✓	
Pewsey: 1.4km (1 mile) off route	0 (0)	68.4 (42½)	✓	✓	2	✓	✓
Wilcot	1.9 (1¼)	70.3 (43¾)		✓	1, 3		
Honeystreet	4.5 (2¾)	74.8 (46½)		✓	1, 2		
All Cannings: 0.9km (½ mile) off route	**3.1 (2)**	**77.9 (48½)**	✓	✓	**1**		

Place	Intermediate distance – km (miles)	Cumulative – km (miles)	Shop	Pub/café	Accomm	Bus	Train
Bishops Cannings: 0.8km (½ mile) off route	4.9 (3)	82.8 (51½)				✓	
Horton Bridge	0.7 (½)	83.5 (52)		✓			
Coate: 1.7km (1 mile) off route	0 (0)	83.5 (52)		✓	1		
Devizes	**4.2 (2½)**	**87.7 (54½)**	✓	✓	**2, 3**	✓	
Rowde: 1.4km (1 mile) off route	2.9 (1¾)	90.6 (56¼)	✓	✓	2, 3		
Lower Foxhangers Farm	0.8 (½)	91.4 (56¾)			1		
Sells Green	1.9 (1¼)	93.3 (58)		✓		✓	
Seend: 0.7km (½ mile) off route	1.5 (1)	94.8 (59)	✓	✓	1, 2	✓	
Seend Cleeve	0.8 (½)	95.6 (59½)		✓			
Semington: 0.4km (¼ mile) off route	**3.6 (2¼)**	**99.2 (61¾)**	✓	✓	**2, 3**	✓	
Melksham: 2.8km (1¾ miles) off route	0 (0)	99.2 (61¾)	✓	✓	2, 3	✓	✓
Hilperton Marsh	4.0 (2½)	103.2 (64¼)	✓			✓	
Hilperton: 2km (1¼ miles) off route	0 (0)	103.2 (64¼)		✓	2, 3	✓	
Trowbridge: 1.9km (1¼ miles) off route	1.0 (½)	104.2 (64¾)		✓	2, 3	✓	✓
Bradford-on-Avon	**3.6 (2¼)**	**107.8 (67)**	✓	✓	**1, 2, 3**	✓	✓
Avoncliff	2.4 (1½)	110.2 (68½)		✓	2, 3		✓
Freshford: 1.5km (1 mile) off route	0 (0)	110.2 (68½)		✓			✓

Place	Intermediate distance – km (miles)	Cumulative – km (miles)	Shop	Pub/café	Accomm	Bus	Train
Limpley Stoke: 0.5km (¼ mile) off route	2.9 (1¾)	113.1 (70¼)		✔	3	✔	
Dundas	**1.5 (1)**	**114.6 (71¼)**	✔	✔		✔	
Brassknocker Basin: 0.5km (¼ mile) off route	0 (0)	114.6 (71¼)		✔	1		
Monkton Combe: 1.5km (1 mile) off route	0 (0)	114.6 (71¼)		✔	2, 3		
Claverton: 0.2km (1/8 mile) off route	0 (0)	114.6 (71¼)					
Bathampton	5.2 (3¼)	119.8 (74½)	✔	✔	2, 3	✔	
Bathford: 1.2km (¾ mile) off route	0 (0)	119.8 (74½)	✔	✔	2, 3	✔	
Bath	**3.7 (2¼)**	**123.5 (76¾)**	✔	✔	**1, 2, 3**	✔	✔
Saltford	8.8 (5½)	132.3 (82¼)	✔	✔	2, 3	✔	
Keynsham	**5.9 (3¾)**	**138.2 (86)**	✔	✔	**2, 3**	✔	✔
Hanham Mill	3 (1¾)	141.2 (87¾)		✔		✔	
Conham (ferry)	3.2 (2)	144.4 (89¾)		✔			
Crew's Hole	1.6 (1)	146 (90¾)		✔			
Bristol	6.1 (3¾)	152.1 (94½)	✔	✔	1, 2, 3	✔	✔

APPENDIX C

Accommodation near the route

Reading
Numerous choices, including B&Bs,
pubs with rooms, and hotels

Theale
The Old Lamb Hotel
tel 0118 930 2357
www.oldlambhotel.co.uk

Sulhamstead
Field Farm Cottage
tel 0118 930 2735
www.bandbwestberkshire.co.uk

Aldermaston Wharf
Comfort Hotel
tel 0118 971 3282
www.comfortreading.co.uk

Holiday Inn
tel 0118 971 4411
www.ihg.com/holidayinn

The Butt Inn
tel 0118 971 3309
www.thebuttinn.biz

Aldermaston
The Hind's Head
tel 0118 971 2194
www.hindsheadaldermaston.co.uk

Midgham
Berkshire Arms
tel 0118 971 4114
www.chefandbrewer.com

West Grange Hotel
tel 01635 273074
www.westgrangehotel.co.uk

Meadow Thatch B&B
tel 0118 971 3819
www.meadowthatch.com

Thatcham
The Swan
tel 01635 862084
www.swanpubthatcham.co.uk

The White Hart
tel 01635 863251
www.thewhitehartthatcham.com

Newbury
Numerous choices, including
campsites, B&Bs, pubs with rooms, and
hotels

Kintbury
The Dundas Arms
tel 01488 658263
www.dundasarms.co.uk

Hungerford
The Bear Hotel
tel 01488 682512
www.oldenglishinns.co.uk

Clevedon House B&B
tel 01488 684730
www.clevedonhousehungerford.co.uk

Honeybones B&B
tel 01488 683228
www.honeybone.co.uk

The Three Swans Hotel
tel 01488 682721
www.threeswans.net

Froxfield
The Pelican Inn
tel 01488 682479
www.pelicaninn.co.uk

Crofton
Crofton Lodge B&B
tel 01672 870328
www.croftonlodge.co.uk

Wolfhall
Suddene Park Farm campsite and B&B
tel 01672 810296
www.suddeneparkfarm.co.uk

Wootton Rivers
The Royal Oak
tel 01672 810322
www.wiltshire-pubs.co.uk

Easton Royal
The Bruce Arms campsite
tel 01672 810216
www.thebrucearms.net

Follets B&B
tel 01672 810619
www.folletsbb.com

Gilden Down B&B
tel 01672 810316

Pewsey
Circles B&B
tel 01672 569390
www.circlesbandb.com

Sharcott Barracks B&B
tel 01672 564112
www.sharcottbarracks.co.uk

Wilcot
The Golden Swan and campsite
tel 01672 562289
www.thegoldenswan.co.uk

Honeystreet
The Barge Inn campsite
tel 01672 851705
www.the-barge-inn.com

Well Cottage B&B
tel 01672 851655
www.well-cottage.org.uk

All Cannings
Little Owls Campsite
01380 848253
www.littleowlscamping.co.uk

Coate
The New Inn campsite
01380 860644
www.newinncoate.co.uk

Devizes
Several choices of B&Bs, pubs with rooms, and hotels

Rowde
George and Dragon
tel 01380 723053
www.thegeorgeanddragonrowde.co.uk

Vine Cottage B&B
tel 01380 728360
www.vinecottagebb.co.uk

Lower Foxhangers Farm
Campsite
tel 01380 828254
www.canalsideholidays.co.uk

Sells Green
Devizes Camping and Caravanning Club Site
tel 01380 828839
www.campingandcaravanningclub.co.uk

The Three Magpies campsite
tel 01380 828389
www.threemagpies.co.uk

Seend
Brookes Farm B&B
www.brookesfarm.com

Cleeve House
tel 01380 827129
www.cleeve-house.com

The Swallows Camping and
Caravan Site
tel 01380 828231
www.theswallowsseend.co.uk

Semington
Bridge House B&B
tel 01225 703281

Newhouse Farm B&B
tel 01380 870349
www.newhousefarmwilts.co.uk

Somerset Arms
tel 01380 870067
www.somersetarmssemington.co.uk

Melksham
Several choices of B&Bs, pubs with
rooms, and hotels

Trowbridge
Several choices of B&Bs, pubs with
rooms, and hotels

Hilperton
The Lion and Fiddle Hotel
tel 01225 776392

Heron's Knoll B&B
tel 01225 752593
www.heronsknoll.co.uk

Bradford-on-Avon
Several choices, including campsites,
B&Bs, pubs with rooms, and hotels

Avoncliff
The Cross Guns
tel 01225 862335
www.crossguns.net

The Railway Studio B&B
tel 01225 865789
www.railwaystudio.co.uk

Limpley Stoke
Limpley Stoke Hotel
tel 01225 723333
www.limpleystokehotel.co.uk

Brassknocker Basin
Campsite
tel 07970 279749
www.brassknockerbasincamping.co.uk

Monkton Combe
The Manor House
tel 01225 723128

Waterhouse Hotel
tel 01225 721999
www.waterhousebath.co.uk

The Wheelwrights Arms
tel 01225 722287
www.wheelwrightsarms.co.uk

Bathampton
Lindisfarne Guest House
tel 01225 466342
www.lindisfarnebath.com

The Old Mill Hotel
tel 01225 858476
www.oldmillbath.co.uk

Wee Grange
tel 01225 445995
www.holidayinbath.com

Bathford
The Cedars B&B
tel 01225 852897
www.thecedarsbath.com

Bath
Lots of choices, including youth hostel, B&Bs, pubs with rooms, and hotels

Saltford
Kendall Guest House
tel 01225 872499
www.kendall-house.co.uk

Prospect Villa B&B
tel 01225 873211
www.prospectvilla.co.uk

Riverside Inn
tel 01225 873862
www.riversideinnsaltford.com

The White House B&B
tel 01225 872167
www.whitehousebath.com

Keynsham
The Crown Inn
tel 0117 986 2150

The Grange Hotel
tel 0117 986 9181
www.grangehotelkeynsham.com

Grasmere Court Hotel
tel 0117 986 2662
www.grasmerecourthotel.com

Manor Lodge Guest House
tel 0117 986 2191
www.manorlodge.co.uk

The Old Manor House Hotel
tel 0117 986 3107
www.oldmanorhousehotel.co.uk

Bristol
Lots of choices, including youth hostel, B&Bs, pubs with rooms, and hotels

APPENDIX D
Useful contacts

About the canal
To learn about the volunteers who saved
the canal, visit:
The Kennet & Avon Canal Trust
tel 01380 721279
www.katrust.org.uk

For canal information (including any
temporary towpath closures), visit:
The Canal & River Trust
tel 0303 040 4040
www.canalrivertrust.org.uk

Tourist information

Bath
tel 0844 847 5256
www.visitbath.co.uk

Bradford-on-Avon
tel 01225 865797
www.bradfordonavon.co.uk

Bristol
tel 0906 711 2191
www.visitbristol.co.uk

Devizes
tel 01380 500276
www.devizes.org.uk

Hungerford
tel 01488 682419
www.hungerford.co.uk

Melksham
tel 01225 707424
www.visit-melksham.com

Newbury
tel 01635 30267
www.visitnewbury.org.uk

Reading
www.livingreading.co.uk

Trowbridge
tel 01225 765072
www.trowbridge.gov.uk

Visit Somerset
tel 01749 835416
www.visitsomerset.co.uk

Visit Wiltshire
tel 01722 323036
www.visitwiltshire.co.uk

Public transport information
For train enquiries contact National Rail
tel 08457 484950
www.nationalrail.co.uk

Traveline is the best resource for checking
bus timetables
tel 0871 2002233
www.traveline.info

Local Wildlife Trusts
Avon Wildlife Trust
tel 0117 917 7270
www.avonwildlifetrust.org.uk

Berks, Bucks & Oxon Wildlife Trust
tel 01865 775476
www.bbowt.org.uk

Wiltshire Wildlife Trust
tel 01380 725670
www.wiltshirewildlife.org

Other contacts
Ramblers Association
tel 020 7339 8500
www.ramblers.org.uk

RSPCA
(for sick, injured or distressed animals or
birds)
tel 0300 1234 999
www.rspca.org.uk

APPENDIX E
Further reading

Berry, Warren *The Kennet and Avon Navigation: A History* (Phillimore, 2009)

Broom, Ian *The Crofton Story* (Wiltshire Archaeological & Natural History Society, 2013)

Chandler, John *Devizes and Central Wiltshire* (Hobnob Press, 2007)

Clew, Kenneth *The Kennet & Avon Canal* (David & Charles, 3rd edn, 1985)

Davison, Steve *The North Wessex Downs* (Hale Books, 2013)

Hackford, Clive *The Kennet & Avon Canal* (The History Press, 2012)

Hackford, Clive *The Kennet & Avon Canal Through Time* (Amberley Publishing, 2009)

Hackford, Clive and Hackford, Helen *The Kennet & Avon Canal From Old Photographs* (Amberley Publishing, 2010)

Lindley-Jones, Peter *Restoring the Kennet & Avon Canal* (The History Press, 2002)

Pevsner, Nikolaus (founding editor) *The Buildings of England*, series of guides by county, including Berkshire, Wiltshire and Somerset (Yale University Press)

NOTES

NOTES

NOTES

NOTES

NOTES

LISTING OF CICERONE GUIDES

Walking in Corsica
Walking in Provence – East
Walking in Provence – West
Walking in the Auvergne
Walking in the Cevennes
Walking in the Dordogne
Walking in the Haute Savoie –
    North & South
Walks in the Cathar Region

GERMANY
Hiking and Biking in the
    Black Forest
Walking in the Bavarian Alps

HIMALAYA
Annapurna
Bhutan
Everest
The Mount Kailash Trek
Trekking in Ladakh
Trekking in the Himalaya

ICELAND & GREENLAND
Trekking in Greenland
Walking and Trekking
    in Iceland

IRELAND
The Irish Coast to Coast Walk
The Mountains of Ireland

ITALY
Gran Paradiso
Sibillini National Park
Shorter Walks in the Dolomites
The Way of St Francis
Through the Italian Alps
Trekking in the Apennines
Trekking in the Dolomites
Via Ferratas of the Italian
    Dolomites: 1&2
Walking in Abruzzo
Walking in Italy's Stelvio
    National Park
Walking in Sardinia
Walking in Sicily
Walking in the Central
    Italian Alps
Walking in the Dolomites
Walking in Tuscany
Walking in Umbria
Walking on the Amalfi Coast
Walking the Italian Lakes
Walks and Treks in the
    Maritime Alps

MEDITERRANEAN
Jordan – Walks, Treks, Caves,
    Climbs and Canyons
The High Mountains of Crete
The Mountains of Greece
Treks and Climbs in Wadi Rum
Walking and Trekking on Corfu
Walking on Malta
Western Crete

NORTH AMERICA
British Columbia
The Grand Canyon
The John Muir Trail
The Pacific Crest Trail

SOUTH AMERICA
Aconcagua and the
    Southern Andes
Hiking and Biking Peru's
    Inca Trails
Torres del Paine

SCANDINAVIA
Walking in Norway

**SLOVENIA, CROATIA
AND MONTENEGRO**
The Islands of Croatia
The Julian Alps of Slovenia
The Mountains of Montenegro
Trekking in Slovenia
Walking in Croatia
Walking in Slovenia:
    The Karavanke

SPAIN AND PORTUGAL
Coastal Walks in Andalucia
Mountain Walking in
    Southern Catalunya
Spain's Sendero Histórico:
    The GR1
The Mountains of Nerja
The Northern Caminos
Trekking through Mallorca
Walking in Andalucia
Walking in Madeira
Walking in Mallorca
Walking in Menorca
Walking in the Algarve
Walking in the Cordillera
    Cantabrica
Walking in the Sierra Nevada
Walking on Gran Canaria
Walking on La Palma
Walking on Lanzarote and
    Fuerteventura

Walking on Tenerife
Walking on the Costa Blanca
Walking the GR7 in Andalucia
Walks and Climbs in the
    Picos de Europa

SWITZERLAND
Alpine Pass Route
The Swiss Alps
Tour of the Jungfrau Region
Walking in the Bernese Oberland
Walking in the Valais
Walks in the Engadine

TECHNIQUES
Geocaching in the UK
Indoor Climbing
Lightweight Camping
Map and Compass
Mountain Weather
Outdoor Photography
Polar Exploration
Rock Climbing
Sport Climbing
The Hillwalker's Manual

MINI GUIDES
Alpine Flowers
Avalanche!
Navigation
Pocket First Aid and
    Wilderness Medicine
Snow

MOUNTAIN LITERATURE
8000 metres
A Walk in the Clouds
Abode of the Gods
Unjustifiable Risk?

For full information on all our
guides, books and eBooks,
visit our website:
www.cicerone.co.uk.

Walking – Trekking – Mountaineering – Climbing – Cycling

Over 40 years, Cicerone have built up an outstanding collection of over 300 guides, inspiring all sorts of amazing adventures.

 Every guide comes from extensive exploration and research by our expert authors, all with a passion for their subjects. They are frequently praised, endorsed and used by clubs, instructors and outdoor organisations.

All our titles can now be bought as **e-books**, **ePubs** and **Kindle** files and we also have an online magazine – **Cicerone Extra** – with features to help cyclists, climbers, walkers and trekkers choose their next adventure, at home or abroad.

Our website shows any **new information** we've had in since a book was published. Please do let us know if you find anything has changed, so that we can publish the latest details. On our **website** you'll also find great ideas and lots of detailed information about what's inside every guide and you can buy **individual routes** from many of them online.

It's easy to keep in touch with what's going on at Cicerone by getting our monthly **free e-newsletter**, which is full of offers, competitions, up-to-date information and topical articles. You can subscribe on our home page and also follow us on **Facebook** and **Twitter** or dip into our **blog**.

Cicerone – the very best guides for exploring the world.

CICERONE

2 Police Square Milnthorpe Cumbria LA7 7PY
Tel: 015395 62069 info@cicerone.co.uk
www.cicerone.co.uk and www.cicerone-extra.com